Familial Integrity

We Are All One Family — the Family of Humanity

LILY AND THE GROUP THROUGH

BEVERLEY BRIGHT STAR

Familial Integrity

We Are All One Family — the Family of Humanity

LILY AND THE GROUP THROUGH

BEVERLEY BRIGHT STAR

LIGHT Technology PUBLISHING

* * *

ISBN-13: 978-1-62233-001-0

Light Technology Publishing, LLC
Phone: 800-450-0985
928-526-1345
Fax: 928-714-1132
PO Box 3540
Flagstaff, AZ 86003
www.lighttechnology.com

Contents

Foreword

We want to thank and welcome all of you to the adventure of reading this book! We sincerely hope that each and every one of you who reads this book over the many years that it will be in print will be both delighted and informed by the many diverse, exciting, and humorous stories included in this manual of the law of one. Again, we devote this and each succeeding volume to the wonderful and glorious people of this Earth, and to all of Earth's future inhabitants. This is a book that is indeed both timeless and timely, both in its very nature and by its contents, which will be enjoyed for eons to come. It is our sincere hope, and with the deepest desire in all of our hearts, that this will mark a turning point in the spiritual evolution of this planet and its restoration to the galactic lineage of nations to which you belong and have belonged to in ages past.

You can rest assured that we will be on the sidelines doing our part to help each and every one of you understand and assimilate this book, and all future volumes, into your minds, your hearts, and your very DNA itself! Make no mistake, this book has the power to change lives — and Earth history, if you will let it!

We hope and pray that that is indeed what will happen along the way of your lives' journeys and sojourns upon this Earth. We welcome you and take you all into our hearts and hope that, someday, we will indeed meet again!

To you, your posterity, and to all People of Earth: *Namasté!*

We want to tell you about a few things that you need to know about this book. In the year that it has taken to bring this book to print, we have observed that certain things have occurred that will change the way the public views this book.

We would also like to say that we have been amenable to the changes in the book. They have not been significant, nor have they altered the intended message of each story. We wish to thank the channel for her persistence, time, and pursuit of excellence in what has been a difficult year for her. She has, indeed, resuscitated her spiritual work and life, and we are very proud of the work she has done so far. This is to acknowledge her and encourage her to always do her best, no matter what the circumstance!

All of you now living in the world in the year 2012 have already been through many things: You have already had a few cataclysms and earthquakes, nuclear power plants that have overheated, fish and whales have been dying, and so on. We have also observed that in this year and the past year, 2011, humans have taken a giant leap forward in their personal ascension processes. Many of you are beginning to take your self-transformation seriously and do some serious groundwork in laying the foundation for the rest of your sojourn upon this planet.

But what we want you all to know is how proud we are of everyone on this planet who has consciously and deliberately moved themselves forward, both by their own effort and by the tremendous efforts of all lightworkers now residing on this planet.

It is with humble gratitude and sublime peace and joy that we, the Sirian Council of 12, thank all of you here, from the bottom of our hearts to yours. The ineffable joy that is on our home planet of Sirius B right now is something that cannot be merely expressed in words. We love you all so much! Remember that we are with you all always, loving and guiding you all toward the noble and transformative end to your lives that you all have so richly earned — and deserve!

— The Sirian Council of 12

Preface

It has been our pleasure to bring this publication to fruition in book form. We know that the channel expressed her wish that it begin in book form first, but since its partial publication in the magazine *Sedona Journal of Emergence!*, we have been pleased to note that the ideas and ideals set forth in the manuscript have gone out into the cosmos of people's minds and hearts.

This has started a chain reaction, known also as the ripple effect, and we are very pleased to note that these ideations, formulas, and such are starting to be felt in the grid and indeed the cosmos itself. This was unanticipated, even by us, and we wish to convey our sincerest gratitude to the channel and her husband for bringing this to such an incredible place so soon. Their activities working with beloved Jeshua and the Elohim of this planet have indeed taught them both how to manifest in the physical as well as spiritual realms. An added element of divine love and joy has helped to propel this forward in a much larger and faster way to a larger arena than we — and others in these outer realms — originally anticipated.

We realize now that the potential of this book may go way beyond all expectation and indeed manifest its proliferation greatly in the next few years, something that we thought would take twenty or more of your years to achieve.

Thank you to all who have come together in the name of the lord and all the universe to bring this about. On Sirius there has been much rejoicing, as this will greatly alter and tremendously speed up the original timeframe for Earth's ascension. Thank you to all for your encouragement and prayers along the way!

— Lily and the Group

, , ,

We look forward today to meeting each and every one of you, both in spirit and in form someday. We wish you all to know that this book project has been planned for many eons of time. We wish you could see the excitement here on our planet, waiting for the release of this great material to planet Earth!

As we await publication, we just want to say that we think after reading, digesting, and processing this book, you will find that the information contained within it will go into the mainframe of your mind and consciousness to enlighten you and pencil into your psyche and soul the required changes that humankind needs and must make for this new millennium and this new age.

We are both overjoyed and pleased that this great work has come to form, bringing Lily's great wisdom, wit, pathos, and humor to page and form in front of the very eyes of the readers, a primer of sorts for the edification of humankind through the annals of time itself.

We encourage all of you to use this information for both education and enjoyment in as many ways as you can. Read each page. Cherish each idea. Put them in your hearts and treasure them as your own. The ideals put forth will, at some point in your spiritual evolution, become inculcated and encoded as part of your mind, your body, and your soul — they will actually become part of you. Then and only then will there be a new world, a new age, and a bright and beautiful future for all of you!

It has been a pleasure and a privilege to bring about this material. The great principles of the law of one have already been implanted and implemented on this great planet many millennia ago on your continents of Mu, Lemuria, and Atlantis. We also want to point out that over a long period of time, these principles were lost to antiquity, and they have only been hinted at in archaeological digging sites around the globe. We wanted to bring the principles back again in a way that humanity could find useful and practical on a daily basis; we wanted to reintroduce this material at a deep level to all who set eyes on these pages.

We and others have embedded these codings deep within the text of each page, each story, bringing each person into a present-moment format as they read and process the new information. This text has been programmed to unlock hidden pathways within each of you to reconnect and reawaken long-buried ancient knowledge held deep within the consciousness of the mass mind of humanity. We know that each person will awaken at his or her own proper time and place and that this book will greatly help in that awakening. It is our heartfelt hope that, with time, these ideas and ideals will spread over the entire Earth, as that was, and still is, our original intent for this material.

God go with you all. And remember, we are here with you now — use us! Namasté and peace.

— Lily and the Sirian Council of 12

Introduction

We are here today to introduce you to a concept that may be unfamiliar to a lot of you. It is a concept called *familial integrity*. We are introducing it into the group consciousness of humankind.

It is a concept that is kept on many other planets and, for some, composes much of the moral bases for their worlds. We introduce it here as a series of teachings. It has much to do with the family unit, yes, but it must be seen as a moral preceptor of sorts, a logo for humanity to move toward, to strive for as an ideal, if you will.

Moving beyond its immediate ramifications, we mean integrity within the family — as this is implicit — more in a sense of what you would call the family of humanity itself. When it moves into this status, it indeed becomes that which will bring stability, peace, and love to the entire planet.

For you see, you are all family to each other, whether you recognize that yet or not. You should begin to see each other — each race, each creed, each country — as one, as the same as what on other planets is called the law of one, because it immediately acknowledges that which is already so. You are one family, in essence, and in every way possible. Even your scientists have acknowledged this — you are family! You are your brother's keeper, and even more than that: He is you and you are he. It can be no other way, for this is the true reality.

Now the principle of familial integrity takes on a whole new meaning, does it not? If this principle were acknowledged in every dealing humans have with each other, think how things would change — and very rapidly! You could no longer leave your brother to starve; deny him adequate food or housing; cheat, lie, or steal from him — or even kill him, because you cannot kill your own brother, your own flesh and blood, your own countryman, if he is fully acknowledged to be the family member that he truly is.

Do you see how such a simple ideal with its recognition and acknowledgment could have such far-reaching propensities and be a catalyst for interpersonal global change between individuals and nations?

So you see what the potentials are for this and where we, and you, are going …

— Lily and the Group
April 4, 2011

1

The Story of Arcturianus

This is a story about a boy named Arcturianus. When he was born his parents named him after one of the stars: Arcturus. Now, Arcturianus was a very odd little fellow. He was very different from the other children. He loved his grandparents very much, and that is not unusual. In fact, he seemed to get along really well with older people. When he was growing up and he would see older people walking along in a mall or a store, he would always run up to them and just hug them. It started to become a bit of a problem, because he was a three- or four-year-old child running up to hug total strangers!

His parents kept asking him why he did it, and he would say, "Mommy, but I know them already" — but, of course, in the much simpler phrasing of a small child, like, "But Mommy, Mommy, I 'member them. That one is Elsie, and that one's Robert. Don't you 'member, Mommy? Don't you 'member?"

"No, I don't, honey," his mother would reply. "Why, they're just strangers. We don't know them. They're not neighbors of ours or anything. But you say you know who they are?"

"Yes, Mommy. They were there at the other place, you know, where we lived before — the big white house with green windows and a big, big yard. Don't you 'member, Mommy?"

"No, honey – I don't. I really don't. You're just imagining things. Now come back over here now and let's go home."

"Oh, okay, Mommy. I'll be good. Don't be mad at me."

"I'm not mad, honey. It's all right. It's all right."

And they would go home every time, and Arcturianus would go and play in his room with his toys. He would feel bad because his parents didn't want him to do talk to strangers like that, and he was a little hurt that they didn't seem to remember anything about their life before like he did. He could see and sense these things very well. It seemed so easy for him.

But as time went by and he got a little older, he not only learned to stop running up to hug elderly people, but he stopped doing it for his own reasons, too. The things that he had seen and sensed were starting to fade away. He even got to a point where he stopped remembering. He couldn't mention anything about it at school because he wanted to be accepted as normal, but deep inside, he never totally lost sight of his memories from an earlier life.

Occasionally, he would have dreams of days in a bygone era when he was a little girl with ringlets in her hair, living in a big white house with a dog, a German shepherd. In the dream, Arcturianus and the dog would run up and down the sidewalks where there was a big expanse of lawns and many mature apple trees, laden with fruit. In the dream, Arcturianus would pick an apple and start running back home, the dog following close behind, protecting her/him. This point in the dream was when Arcturianus always woke up. In the dream, he/she never made it back to the house. It always ended there abruptly. Arcturianus would wake up in a sweat every time and his heart would be racing, almost like it was a nightmare. He always woke up with a feeling of dread and panic. He just couldn't figure it out.Now Arcturianus, unbeknown to everybody, including himself, had been born with a connection to the stars. He had just previously been through an incarnation on Sirius, the Dog Star, and he knew he had been there with his mother. But there was no way that his mother could understand this, because she herself did not remember being there, nor would she have been open to that possibility. Being so young, Arcturianus did not know why he was having these dreams, and there was no one in his world who could tell him. He was a bit of a stubborn boy, so when people told him that his dreams and visions were nonsense, he insisted that he wasn't making it up and would get a little mad. To him the dreams were totally real, but everybody else just dismissed them as childhood fantasies. So Arcturianus grew up thinking that no one understood or believed him, and this hurt him. When he got a little older he stopped telling anyone about his dreams and visions because, for one thing, it just wasn't worth it — and for another, no one would have believed him. The nightmares that he used to have faded away as he grew up, but the one recurring nightmare in which he was a girl had always unnerved him. There just seemed to be no explanation for it, and it always threw him into a bit of a private panic for an hour or so after he woke up from it.

One day after he was grown and had moved out on his own, Arcturianus decided to consult a psychic concerning his childhood visions and nightmares. This psychic told him an incredible story: She told him that the dreams and visions had indeed been deep remembrances of former lives on Earth and Sirius and that his mother had indeed been there with him, although she had no memory of any of it. She also told him that he was also psychic but didn't know it, and she explained to him why the visions had been so strong: because they had actually not been visions. He had astral-traveled back and forth to Sirius on the nights that he had had the dreams! Another interesting and mind-boggling thing she told him was that he could astral travel consciously if he wanted to, and she could teach him how to do it. Arcturianus did not know what to think about that and told the psychic that he would let her know.

But by far the most interesting facet of the psychic session was what she told him about the nightmare. If you remember, it was always the same one, in the same sequence of events: As the little girl, Arcturianus would be walking down the sidewalk in front of a neighborhood with the dog, and then this sickening feeling of dread would come over him and the dream would end. Here's what the psychic told him: The dream was something that had happened in a previous life here on Earth. When he had been the little girl walking innocently down the street with her dog, he had witnessed something he shouldn't have. A man from the neighborhood had come running down the street covered in blood, and when he reached the little girl and her dog, he just reached out and stabbed her in broad daylight, and then dragged her to a back alley where he proceeded to kill her. There was no rhyme or reason to it. It turned out that the man from down the street was mentally ill and had gone on a killing spree, and he had attacked anyone he encountered. The nightmare had always ended right before the girl saw the man to spare Arcturianus the details of his previous death experience.

Arcturianus sat there for a long time after the psychic left and tried to process the astounding and dismaying news of his previous incarnation as a female. He had always had a deep, deep sense, though, when he saw the girl in the dreams, that he *was* the girl, and it had turned out to be correct. He went home that day with a renewed sense of self-worth. He was not crazy, nor had he been making things up as he had been accused of as a child. He had kept all of this buried inside of him; it was always a source of deep pain, rejection, and anger that came from never being understood or even believed, and from having to totally bury something that was so integral to his well-being and to who he was as a person. Now he knew that there was a real explanation for everything that he had experienced and why he had experienced it.

At this point he decided to "come out of the closet" and tell his mother and everyone who knew him what the psychic had told him. They were shocked to hear that things like past lives and astral travel were real. They were even more shocked to learn the details of the horrible death Arcturianus had suffered at the hands of a crazy person. But the most curious thing to all of them, especially his mother, was that he had been a girl in a previous life. Not only did Arcturianus's mother not know about previous lives, but she didn't know that a person could be a member of the opposite sex and not remember it. But she loved her son and believed he wasn't lying to her. She apologized to him for not believing him when he was little, and they reconciled. After that, their relationship became deeper and much closer than it had ever been. And Arcturianus decided to take lessons from the psychic after all!

2

The Hares

Once upon a time, there were three hares named Gertrude, Penelope, and Harry. They came from a huge clan and were members of the hare family, a larger species of the rabbit family.

The clan lived close to a waste treatment plant, but it had not always been so. When the hare family established their clan burrow, the surrounding area had been pristine, beautiful, and far out in nature — but this is where the story of the history of the hare clan took a turn. The idea that their family could live in peace and harmony on Earth was no more.

When the waste plant was built, no one in their great family knew what it was or what to do. "Do we abandon our burrows and leave our homeland behind, or do we stay here and try to live as we have always lived?" they wondered. And a great discussion developed among them: "Let us all come together and make a decision." After much thought, many ideas, and intense emotions, it was decided that they would stay and wait it out — they would wait and see.

Now, this waste treatment plant was very efficient and

functioned well. "Let's build in this beautiful place out by the woods," the people had all said, "and then we won't be disturbing nature very much at all!" But as the land was being mapped and surveyed, the people discovered the large field of rabbit burrows. It seemed to be the edge of a large complex of them. The plant was not considered close enough to ever be a threat to the wildlife of the area because of a system of checks and balances that were in place; in accordance with state and federal regulations, the land was declared safe. So the construction proceeded and the plant became operational.

The hares did not understand what was happening, but they accepted the inevitability of it and moved on with their lives. And all was fine for a while, but then they started noticing foul smells that seemed to be coming from the side of the burrow neighborhood that was nearest to the plant. Some of them ventured closer to the area and were almost overwhelmed by noxious fumes coming into some of the burrows, and they ran back quickly.

One of the inquiring hares was Penelope, one of our three rabbit friends. She came running back to her friends and gasped. "I don't know what it is, but something smelled really bad — I think I'm feeling sick!" she said. She fell down and lay on her side, breathing heavily. "Don't go over there! Don't go over there!" she blurted out. And then she was silent. Harry crept over to look more closely at his friend and noticed that she was hardly breathing at all. Then she slipped into a coma and died.

A great sadness came over the entire burrow clan. The other rabbits who had been with Penelope also got very sick and died within hours. The clan had another meeting in which they decided to close off the section of their land that was nearest to the plant, so that was done. And for a long while it seemed to work — there were no more deaths for what seemed like a long time, and all seemed to get back to normal. But Harry and Gertrude missed Penelope very much. She had been the one who could always make them laugh, and she had been the leader in fun and games when they were younger. Playful and adventurous, she could always think of a new game. "Sweet Miss Penelope — we miss her so much! What happened to her? Why did she have to die? She is so very missed around here. It's just not the same!" they cried.

Then one day everyone woke up to shaking — the earth was moving! Dirt was falling all around them. "Run, quick! Run for your life!" Harry shouted at Gertrude. But Gertrude was not moving — she was buried under a huge pile of dirt as the burrow collapsed in on her. Then, just as suddenly as it had begun, the earth stopped shaking. Harry started digging furiously to uncover his dear friend. He quickly uncovered her face, yelling, "Gertrude! Gertrude! Wake up! Wake up!" But his friend lay motionless. Harry pushed and nudged her a bit. Suddenly, one of Gertrude's huge ears twitched, and her eyes opened. She was still alive! She was going to be okay after all!

The two hares frolicked and played in their happiness in finding each other alive, and it so happened that they were so excited that they ran very far away in the joy of the moment — far away into the forest where they had played as children. So great was their joy that they ran with abandon, hither and yon, uphill and downhill. But when Harry looked, he saw that the shadows caused by the sun had grown long. So they decided they had better go back home, and they hurried back to the clan.

But as they approached, they smelled something awful again — even worse than before. They became scared and stopped right where they were, still a far distance away from the burrow colony. They peered over the small hill that they had hidden in behind a large thicket, and that's when they saw something they would never forget: Their entire clan was lying scattered about dead. Harry and Gertrude could still smell a hint of the fatal fumes, so they knew they could not go any closer.

Horrified and fighting back tears, they slowly backed up and bolted away again, this time in fear and pain. Their entire family was gone now — they were the only two left. Gone was the intense joy of the previous moments and hours. They ran far away again. They huddled together all night, trying to forget the ugly sight, but there was no comfort for either of them, and they felt lost, inside and out. Occasionally big tears fell out of their eyes, and they would rub them away for each other.

At dawn the next day, they awoke and made a decision: They had to go warn the other clans about this great disaster. They also wanted to find a new family, so off they went.

They had to travel far, and the journey was difficult, lasting many days and weeks. After one exhausting day of climbing hill after hill, they came to a great meadow area in a small valley. Looking below, they noticed burrows that looked like the ones they had left behind. It looked like they had found their new family!

, , ,

A Closer Look

So far, the story of the hares has been one of family, friends, and the natural balance and flow of life on our Earth, has it not? The hare colony had lived in harmony with nature and humanity from time immemorial. So what changed? Their simple existence had flourished and abounded along in accordance with the dictates of nature and of their species. Each generation had a certain natural flow of one to the other — the natural order of life here. So what came along to change this? Can we find the causation?

Unity through Symbiosis

Let's look at the story more closely. When you have, as you do on this planet, as many species as you have here, in order for all of them to live in harmony, they must interlock together, each one depending on the other and so on. Your word is "symbiotic." In symbiotic relationships, as you all know, not only do species interlock but they depend on each other for their very existence — one *blesses* the other by being there. So there is unity through symbiosis, is there not? This is an interesting dichotomy, and at the same time, a simple and extremely complex process — all the while being a virtual and literal genius of design, form, and function, to name just a few. The Creator of this planet intended this to be so. It is another example, inherent in all nature, of our "unity by design" principle, is it not?

Harmony Destroyed

So in our hare story, the large rabbit family had lived in harmony, as all animal families do — in harmony and peace, all things leading to each other, dependent on each other in the positive way that families are meant to be. So what happened? Of course, as we know from our story, a waste treatment plant was built nearby. Now we don't want our readers to jump to the automatic conclusion that this story is about making the humans the bad guys — it's not. That is not the purpose of this story, as you will soon see.

Earlier in our parable, there was a minor leak at the plant that killed several of the hares, and the rabbits learned to stay away from that part of their burrow complex. The humans discovered the leak and fixed it, and the plant was apparently able to operate for quite a while with no more accidents. For all intents and purposes, the leak was permanently fixed, was it not? But then a worst-case scenario occurred: the earthquake!

Now, this was something that was unanticipated by the planners and builders of the waste treatment plant. The plant had not been built in a traditional earthquake area, and none of the surveys or environmental impact studies had indicated that an earthquake might occur in this region. So they had done their homework, and done all the things that a responsible company would have done. They had also seen the large rabbit community a mile away but, with all the safety precautions that were taken with the design and construction of the treatment plant, they figured that if any small leak occurred, they could contain and fix it quickly with minimal damage to the surrounding community and ecosystem. All was done properly and in accordance with the regulations in place at the time. The planners/builders and the surrounding community felt that they had taken all the precautions that they could, and that everything would be fine. But then the earthquake happened. Hares have a family structure in the way animals often do. The babies are often raised by the entire clan, needing their mothers for only a short time. And hares in particular are born with very large hind legs, large ears, and a keen sense of smell. They also have sensitive noses and whiskers for finding the tender parts of plants and roots.

This particular clan had established itself in an area that had enough green fields and surrounding meadows to sustain a large colony of rabbits. However, when the treatment plant was built nearby, the hares assessed the situation and decided to try to stay, never knowing the real danger of doing so. All would have been fine, technically, except for that extremely unforeseen circumstance of nature — the earthquake.

Hare Communities and Human Communities

So you have a rabbit community living next to a human community, and both have needs. The humans, by way of their immense numbers, have pressed far out into nature with their needs. And the hare community has a need to keep the balance of nature as natural as possible, as they have always done. Now, both humans and rabbits tend to have a lot of babies, and there are similarities overall, but by and large, human communities have a tendency to take over wherever they are. Cities grow larger and larger, and large cities in particular have large *everything*. The consequences of the "everything" that comes with them are very large too.

"Good Neighbor" Policy

The waste treatment plant was built on the outskirts of a very large city, and the plant was a fair size too. So when the earthquake happened, the consequential impact felt by nature was also very large. This story is not meant to downplay the impact that an earthquake would have had on the nearby city, but to be a reminder of what can happen to the other living families on Earth — the other inhabitants who share this Earth with us, along with the human impact and what it means to them and their futures. What are they to do? Where can they go, really? And what should our "good neighbor" policy be?

If, for instance, being a good neighbor means looking out for each other, then were we really looking out for our neighbors, the animals? Is it about our responsibility to each other? If it is, then how could we go about looking out for our animal friends? Could we possibly find other more eco-friendly technologies that would not hurt the surrounding ecosystems under *any* circumstances? Would that be being a good neighbor? We are suggesting that it would be — a win-win situation for *all* concerned. That way the hares wouldn't have suffered the loss of their entire colony.

Thinking about Others

Certainly in a natural disaster situation, there would still have been losses, even if the humans had been good neighbors, but only part of the hare family would have died — not the entire clan. And the answer to the question, "Where could they have gone?" would have become a moot point, would it not have? Of course, they could technically have moved their large community somewhere else. But as we all know, the encroachment of humanity upon the planet proves that at some point there is nowhere else to move. So what could be done here? As good neighbors, we must think of all the members of an area — not just ourselves. This, we think, could and should be inherent in any good-neighbor policy.

It is just that usually nobody ever thinks to give our other neighbors a voice, do they? What would happen if they did? Would this really be as difficult or as expensive as we are afraid that it would be? What if, when things like power plants or waste treatment plants or other projects were first proposed, we could all look at other options and choose what was best for the environment? Wouldn't that be better for all concerned? We know that in some places around the globe, these kinds of discussions are taking place, and that is very good. What we would like to see is for these kinds of discussions to become the policy that the entire planet adopts, to become the way it is always done. Then situations like the unfortunate one with the hare population could be avoided. If these other possibilities are never explored, how can we ever know what kind of a planet we can really have?

Changing the Elements: Giving Everyone a Voice

We have given the hare story of how the rabbits were trying to have their own lives, hurting no one, and wanting nothing more than to live out their days in peace and in harmony with all things. This story is about how all living entities on Earth should learn to live: in symbiosis and harmony with each other. It's about how one, if not living in peace or harmony, can be harmful to another.

And as this actually *is* just a story, let us pretend that — as all fables go — we can change the elements in the story if we choose. So let's say that the hare community grew so large that it started to encroach on the life around it. And then let's say that the hares were so numerous that they would break into people's yards and eat up whole gardens at a time — that they were everywhere, burrowing into people's yards and taking over. What would *we* want to say to *them*? Would we know what to do? We would have meetings and committees about what to do about the rabbit problem, wouldn't we?

What if, in our fable, we could send an appointed committee to talk to the rabbits? How would that conversation go? It might go something like this: "We notice that there are so many of you that you are creating tremendous havoc in our own human community. Can we work together to find solutions that are agreeable to both of us? We don't want to criticize or take sides, but this is really getting out of hand! Let's see if we can work together to solve this for both sides. Let's try to make this a win-win situation for all concerned and think outside of the box — instead of coming up with the usual solutions, such as resorting to violence. Can we talk about other options?" You get the drift.

So then, with the shoe on the other foot, what do you think the rabbit community would like to say to us, given the original version of this story? If they could talk to us, what would they say at the onset of the construction of the waste treatment plant? Would they have wanted a voice in the placement of it? Perhaps they would not have wanted it built so close to their already established homes. Or when the first leakage occurred, wouldn't they have wanted more accountability and an investigation into the deaths of a few of their members? Wouldn't they have demanded better solutions and answers from us?

And since this is a parable, what if the plant was not a waste treatment plant, but a nuclear plant? Let's say that the first error occurred from an unforeseen human element. Wouldn't the hare community have wanted a voice then? What could have been the consequences, then, of a nuclear plant involved in the unforeseen natural event — the earthquake? Would there even have been any of them left to have lodged a complaint? Probably not!

The Council Fire

In this fable, the hares — representing the animal kingdom — should have an equal voice to speak for themselves. Having that voice would mean they would be at the council fire as equals and would therefore have equal rights as members of the committee and be viable and valuable adjuncts in all decisions made at that council fire. Therefore, in our fable, they would also be as family — as brothers, as equals — to any and every other member seated around that proverbial fire.What words do you imagine they might want to say? Would they turn to the other council members (humans) and ask why something with such dangerous potential to kill would even have been imagined? Why would this nuclear plant have been built in the first place since it was only, after all, a steam-generating plant? And why couldn't something simpler and less dangerous have been built for far less money for that purpose so that in the event of an unforeseen natural event such as an earthquake, both in local areas and around the globe, only the plant would have had to have been rebuilt? There would never be any danger to *anyone* — no one on Earth would ever have to die!

Giving Earth a Voice

Wouldn't it be interesting to see what Earth itself would have to say if it had a voice? Or the oceans — do you wonder what they might have to say if they were sitting at that council fire with the hares and the rest of us? We wonder if people have ever thought of nature or the natural world in that way. It would be very interesting, would it not? Perhaps our readers could each have their own visualization of that meeting or that council fire. Would yours be like a business meeting, with donuts and coffee being served? Who would the presenter be? Or would your visualization be more childlike and whimsical, like a true fairy tale: "Once upon a time, in a land far, far away, there was a fair damsel whose only friends were the animals, the fairies, and the gnomes ..." Or would there indeed be, as in a traditional council fire, a magnificent intertribal meeting of the clans, elders, and representatives of the many nations, complete with ceremonies, chanting, prayers, and dancers in full costume and the passing of a medicine stick — a grand and solemn council whose honor it would be to sit at. And can you, the reader, see yourself there? What would your question be? What message of great import would you wish to convey? What would be the pouring forth of your heart, your mind, your passion, your soul?

Changing the Elements Again: Different Perspectives

We told you how the two rabbits had come home to find that their home, family, and friends had been destroyed, and how devastated they were. They ran away, journeying long and far before finally coming to a place where they could make a new home. Now, we want to remind you, dear readers, that this is a fable, so here is a different side of the story.

What if we go back and rewrite the story, but this time we do it in such a fashion that the hares are not hares anymore, but instead a den of jackals?

Jackals have a very close-knit family system, much like wolves do. Let's say the jackals had their den within a fairly close proximity to the plant. When the first accident happened — the leakage — the jackals, smelling it, ran far enough away and did not get poisoned. But let's say that, in their den, there were some jackal pups that were too close to the plant, and because these pups were asleep and very small, they were accidentally poisoned. We have to ask ourselves: Do we really care about baby jackals and whether they are safe or not? The bigger question is: Do we care about them as much as we cared about the hare community being decimated, first one way and then another? By this we mean that hares are fairly cute and you care about them, but baby jackals just don't compare to baby hares, now do they? Not even close! Could it be that there's a bit of a prejudice there because one animal is perceived to be more worthy than another? Although we know that hares can be pests and a nuisance, they are not perceived as vicious predators like jackals.

And what would you think if we were dealing with insects? Would you care about *their* lives if we were talking about ants or scorpions? You probably would not care that much, certainly not as much as you do about the hares, would you? We know it is pretty hard to get worked up over a colony of ants dying. So is there a big difference from one species to another concerning how you would feel if their lives were in jeopardy? Probably.

But we want you to think this over, dear readers, and try to understand that in creation, each creature, large and small, is important to the larger scheme of things — no matter how you may personally perceive or feel about them or their species. We are writing this addendum to the story because it is a very difficult dilemma. Is it not?

No matter what we think, all life is precious and important. So we are throwing you all a gauntlet here, intended to make you think about these interesting side issues to the story about the hares. This is not a story intended to have any kind of an ending, and we left it open-ended on purpose. So we invite all of you, dear readers, to enjoy discussing and debating these provocative — and sometimes unanswerable — issues.

Gertrude and Harry Find a New Home

The two remaining hares, Gertrude and Harry, had run away, frightened, from their burrow community. After many days of travel, they had found a new home — a new community of hares just like them. We will take you there now.

Having just arrived at the edge of another large community, Harry and Gertrude slowly crept down the hill and stood waiting for a fellow hare to see them. As the two were waiting, a large brown-and-white hare came hopping by from behind them and addressed them, saying, "Who are you? I've never seen you before. What are you doing here?"

"Don't be alarmed," Harry replied. "We're not here to hurt you. We're scared too. We have come a long distance to find others of our species because our home burrows were wiped out by a pestilence and an earthquake that befell our community. Our entire family was killed, and we had to leave our home and find a new one. May we stay here? We're awfully tired."

The new hare replied, "I'm sorry. I didn't mean to be so short with you, but I'm old and crusty these days. It's just that you startled me, that's all. Hello, I'm Reginald and I'm actually the rabbit who handles newcomers. You are very welcome here! Come, let me show you around. I'll introduce you to everybody. Follow me."

Reginald led the way and they hopped around the community. Everybody was curious about who the new rabbits were and where they had come from, and Reginald gave Gertrude and Harry a newsy update on each family. "Mary and Bertie over here, they've had twelve little ones, you know, but sadly only ten remain. But you know how it is when your children wander off like that — it's too easy to get into trouble. Oh, and Eleanor and Mark, they run the general store where you can get things. Oh, and you'll want to find yourself a home, or you can make one for yourselves — whichever you prefer. Now, you just make yourselves at home, and if you need anything, just let me know. I'm in the burrow right over there in the middle."

Gertrude and Harry just nodded their heads. They didn't know what to think. This community of hares was not like the one they had been used to at all! A general store — what was that? Their old neighborhood was the way they thought all hare communities were — a very simple, no-frills lifestyle. No one in their old home would have walked them around introducing them to everyone. They had to admit, though, that it was kind of nice. In their old neighborhood, everyone looked out for their own family and pretty much kept to themselves. But here … here was something different. They decided to give it a chance.

They had nowhere else to go, really, and would learn to make the best of it. They could adapt. That is the one thing they had learned in their long journey from their old home to here — how to adapt to new circumstances. Because of the circumstances imposed on them by the disaster, they had become good at coping — coping without their beloved family and friends, whom they still missed very much. They still were in shock about the whole thing, but what could they do? Their lives had been affected forever. There was no going back, ever. Harry and Gertrude had found a new home, yes, but they had also found out that this hare community was very different from theirs, and they were not sure what to do about it. They looked at each other and decided that, since they were tired, they would just hole up in a nearby vacant burrow for a couple of days to see how it would go. "A strange community," they thought, and went to sleep.

Early in the morning they were awakened by some noises outside their burrow. There was someone rustling and bustling around up at the top. Peering carefully over the top of their new burrow, Gertrude and Harry looked out to see a large white-and-brown-haired funny-looking hare with glasses and an overcoat. They both realized it was Reginald, there to deliver some carrots along with turnip greens and a small cabbage.

"Well, hello! Good morning to you both. I trust you slept well. I brought the morning groceries for you," Reginald said.

"You did? What are groceries?" Gertrude asked.

"Well, it's the food — the carrots and so forth."

Harry and Gertrude looked at him strangely. "Well, in our old home we were all pretty much on our own. Nobody ever came around to give us stuff. We were pretty much into the natural way. It's what we were taught," explained Harry.

Reginald hunkered over his little cart, looking for something. Then he stood up and put his hands on his hips and laughed. "Oh, you're from one of those old-fashioned communities down south of here. We've heard tales of how spartanly you all live, with everybody fending for themselves. We're a lot more progressive here. Why, when I was a young hare, my mother ran the country store with all the vegetables. You see, we think we should all be helping one another, so different hares are assigned different jobs to help out the whole group of us. That way more things can get done around here. Don't you see? Besides, we all take turns doing it, so this week it was my job to take all the morning carrots around. Then there's another group that goes out to get the carrots every day. We each have our job assignments that rotate each week, and that way we help each other."

"Well, we helped each other, sort of, in our old home. We were kind of on our own — each rabbit for himself — and we thought that's all there was, that's all," said Gertrude.

"Well, then I guess that does seem to make a difference. It's just in the way you look at it, missy. It's just what you're used to, that's all. Now look over here — which ones do you want?"

Gertrude took two carrots and an onion top. "Thank you," she said.

"Okay then. I'll see you both tomorrow. Got to get the rest of the food delivered ..." Reginald's voice trailed away.

Both Gertrude and Harry went over and picked which carrots they wanted and started munching. Hares take a long time to eat, so this took a while. They just did not know what to think of their new community. It was so different! But Reginald seemed nice enough and very friendly, so they decided to stay for a while. Maybe after a while they could go looking for another one that was more like what they were used to, but they weren't sure if they could find one. After all, it had taken so long to find this one. So they munched and talked and munched and talked some more. "Well," they decided, "let's make the best of it!"

Now, it just so happened that there was a fair coming to Harry and Gertrude's new neighborhood — remember, this is a fable! — and all their new neighbors went out to see it. So they went along with some of their new friends, and they had a good time riding all the rides and swinging on the big flowered seesaw with canopies and flags all over it. It was a gay sight and they had a gay time! Everyone came back with their bags full of popcorn and candy sticks.

Harry and Gertrude had never seen or heard of a fair before, but they actually had a good time.

After everybody went to bed, they stayed up late talking. "You know, this isn't a traditional hare community, but they do know how to get together and have fun around here, don't they?" commented Gertrude.

“They sure do,” said Harry, munching on the last of the popcorn.

“You know, Harry, I sure wish we had had some of these things in our old hare community. Since we grew up there, we thought that was all there was — that that was what hares did — to just have that very simple life. But looking back now, I wonder … I wonder if it was okay for us back then? We were happy with our old life and we didn’t know there was any other way to be a hare. We thought that hares were always supposed to be the way we were, to live life as a hare should. We never realized that any other way was possible, or that there were hare communities that were any different. We took it for granted that there was no other way for hares to be. And now we see that there is, and it’s okay. These are nice folks around here who care about each other, help each other, and go out and have fun sometimes. They’re okay too. I guess there’s more than one way to be a hare, and we’ve been part of both. So let’s stay and live here. We can adapt and change if we try. I know we can. Do you agree, Harry?”

“Yup yup. I think you’re right,” he managed to say in between munches and swallows.

“We should just stay here and become a part of this community. We are all one family, after all. There may be old-fashioned hares and progressive hares, and hares that go around putting on county fairs, but I’ll say one thing for sure: In the end, we’re all still of the hare family. After all, we’re more alike than we are different!”

Harry finally finished chewing, and they hugged each other in agreement and friendship.

So Gertrude and Harry stayed with their newfound friends and learned a different way to be hares. They found that they liked the new way of living after all. They settled down and had a little family of their own, and all was well.

3

The Bridge: Communication with Respect, Chastening with Love

Once there was an engineer in a country called All-Era who was building a bridge. This bridge was designed to span across a piece of land from a high plateau to an adjoining one on the other side of a deep chasm. This engineer and the others had designed this bridge to be a new feat of engineering, the newest and latest thing in technical design and expertise.

Now, this man had a fellow engineer who was usually taciturn, but occasionally would add a comment here and there about what do for the construction of the bridge and how it was proceeding. When they reached a certain point in the construction, this quiet fellow saw a minor but crucial flaw that had occurred — not in the design insomuch as the implementation of that design on the building of the bridge itself — so he voiced his opinion.

Construction on that part of the bridge had already begun in earnest. However, our *quiet* guy suddenly became very animated, insisting that the bridge was being constructed in error. He corrected the men building it, saying, "You must take this part down. You built it with great enthusiasm, and I know this was a lot of work, but you did it incorrectly. This portion of the bridge has a new design being implemented. I've seen your high standards and I know you want it to be right, but it needs to be taken down and rebuilt in this section. Thank you."

Naturally, the builders didn't want to admit that they had done their work wrong, nor did they want to start that section over. But because the engineer had approached them courteously and with respect — and because they know that ultimately the bridge *did* need to be built correctly — they tore down that section and rebuilt it.

It came to pass that when the bridge was finished, there was high praise from the press and the media about the brilliance of the new design. In particular, they praised the portion of the bridge that had been rebuilt — not knowing that it had been — saying that the new design would add extra strength, flexibility, and durability, contributing much to the safety and practicality of the bridge. They also added how much money would be saved in the long run. There was even talk of possibly adding the new unique design of that particular portion to all future bridge designs.

Analysis and Moral of the Story

Now of course there is a moral to this story, but do you know what it really is? What *really* contributed the most to the successful completion of it? Was it the bridge design itself? Or was there another extremely important factor in the structure's successful completion? The design was brilliant, but it was the way one of the engineers approached the builders that was most important. He did chasten them, but he did so with respect and honor for what they had already accomplished and all the hard work they had already put into it. His respectful reproach persuaded the workers to make the improvement, even though it was new and different. And that improvement became cornerstone in the accomplishment of a new and better way to build bridges. Because the engineer approached the builders in the way that he did — instead of creating enmity and resistance — he engendered their cooperation and respect, resulting in a better bridge for everyone.

We Are the Bridge

This story points, at first glance, to a new *bridge* construction, does it not? The bridge is all of you, for you are ever under construction, are you not? You are sometimes in need of repairs and sometimes in need of a redesign. Are you not all like this at times? As you go through your lives, is it not necessary sometimes to tear down a part of what has already been constructed, only to rebuild that part? Of course, you often are not wont to do that, as it is perceived to be kind of a pain to do it. The perception is that even a minor overhaul of yourself would just be too much trouble, so you avoid having to do it — until, many times, your life forces you to! But when and if, through kindness or unkindness, a chastening in your life does occur, you should tear down that section and set about rebuilding it — isn't that true? So if you do as they did in our story, that section, that part of you, would begin to glow brighter, be more in balance, and would be able to understand and forgive more, would it not?

So the whole bridge becomes better and brighter, with renewed strength and vigor for the weight that it must hold, becoming a beacon of construction and design — perhaps even a new blueprint for the future of bridges themselves, all because the engineer had the courage to chasten with respect and love at the proper time. Also the construction crew, being thus approached, humbled themselves enough to see that it would be worth tearing down and rebuilding a portion of the bridge if that meant making it better and more in alignment with the perfect plan for the entire project.

Respect and Appreciation

Everyone was able to see the beauty of the innovative design of the bridge because of *how* the engineer had approached the construction crew. Notice that he didn't just harp on them, or jump in and berate them, making them feel stupid and worthless. He knew that endless and negative criticism was not the way to approach them. When there is criticism of this type — punitive and accusatory — it is not *communication with respect*, is it? It shows no respect or appreciation for the work already completed, does it? The construction crew had done a very good job on what they had already gotten done, and it was only right that this be acknowledged, correct? So the engineer approaching them with respect and real appreciation in his mind and heart got the job done.

Familial Integrity: All about Family

How does this example tie in with our theme of familial integrity? First and foremost, had the job not proceeded very well up to that point? You could say that the construction crew had already built previous sections of the bridge with integrity, had they not? So at this point, the bridge, as all bridges must have, had the *structural integrity* needed to hold it together, to be strong as a bridge should be, is that not true? And when the architect approached the building crew with respect and appreciation, can you see that he approached them with the same care that he would have if he was having to correct his own son or daughter — gently, carefully, and with respect for their feelings and acknowledgement of work already done well?

His approach to his crew was as if they were family, was it not? And the building crew, thus approached, reacted in a more thoughtful and positive way than perhaps they would have, had his approach been negative, accusatory, and unduly harsh. Because of this, they felt as if the project was also theirs — it was as much *their* bridge as it was the architect's.

Diversity within Unity

There was cooperation and respect felt on both sides. Each one relied on the other — the architects to survey, map, and design the bridge, and construction crews to bring it forth into reality. Each is equal to the other, both acknowledging the contribution of the other, much as family members — each different from the other but cooperating as a whole unit, *diversity within unity*. Family members are different, but they all know that together they form a clan of sorts. Large or small, families care about each other and treat each other with respect. They are different but are like spokes in a wheel — all are needed to form the wheel so that it can turn and function properly. Some family members are the spokes; others, the hub; some are the rims holding all the spokes together; and still others, the shaft on which the entire wheel turns.

So we have integrity, and we have family. The unity and strength that a family has, coupled with treating each other with integrity, both operating and joining together for the future completion of this bridge, gives us familial integrity — unity, cooperation, respect, and integrity. The bridge was built with integrity, mirroring the structural integrity that every bridge must have.

The Bridge: An Engineering Marvel

Now, let's look at another aspect of this story. When people talk about the use of pinions and sinews in regard to the construction industry, to what are they usually referring? Usually they are talking about the tensile strength of a structure, its gears and levers and so on that comprise the moving parts of a structure or bridge, especially one that is over a river where a portion of it lifts itself to allow for passing boats. Right here we would like to point out what all designers know: that the bridge itself is a whole unit unto itself, almost like a living thing once it is constructed, especially in bridges such as the Golden Gate Bridge. Each facet of the bridge's pinions and sinews is dependent on the others for strength and support. So any variation in the design or construction of a bridge would affect the structure as whole, would it not? Each section upholds the other, strengthening the other parts and working as a well-designed, well-constructed, well-oiled piece of machinery should. This is the original intent of the bridge itself, from blueprint to the finished design. And it can truly be a work of art — an engineering marvel.

Chastening with Love: An In-depth Look

In our story, the underlying theme is one of chastening with love. What does that mean exactly, chastening with love? In the story, the one engineer had to stop and gently upbraid the men in the construction crew about the way in which they had started to implement the construction of a certain crucial portion of the bridge. Remember that the way he approached them was *with love*. So what does "with love" truly mean in this circumstance? Let's try to further explain what exactly we mean by "love" here.

Love in this instance can be defined and known by its fruits of kindness, compassion, and patience. The engineer approached the crew not with anger and harsh criticism but with gentle honesty and truth. It is true that truth is truth in any given moment, but supporting that truth with the softening effect of these two added components enables the hearers of criticism to keep their hearts open in order to hear more clearly and with more impact. When one feels upbraided and criticized, it is natural for both the heart and the mind to "close their wings," so to speak, as a way of involuntarily avoiding injury or hurt. This subconscious tendency to close up is a common occurrence in all of us, but as psychologists well know, it produces a block and greatly hampers the communication process. Far from opening up communication, it sometimes literally shuts it down — the opposite of what the you need in that moment.

Therefore, the love aspects — kindness, gentleness, compassion, patience, empathy, and understanding — open up communication at precisely the vital moment that it is needed. So instead of thinking of love and kindness as weak or unnecessary, please be aware that these are not weaknesses but great strengths. They show and engender respect, do they not? *Communication with respect* — this is what is vitally necessary in all relationships.

Unity by Design: The Human Body

Now we want to introduce another concept: unity by design. This simply means that the original bridge conceptualization of humanity was that humankind's original intent and design was one of unity. The body itself is a good example of this. Each part was designed to go with and be part of the other parts to make up the whole — a living and breathing receptacle for the soul. The eyes depend on the brain to perceive the image; they depend on how far apart they are placed in the head for the merging of a bifocal image; they depend on the way the head moves to see in many directions. Then the head depends on the neck to move it, and all elements of the body depend on the heart and lungs to move life through them and so on. So the body itself was truly designed with "unity by design" in mind.

Unity and the Family

So now, what about the societal structures of how human beings interact with each other? Let's take a look at that. We have already touched on the unity of the family/clan. Each person is an individual within the clan unit (note the root of the word "unity" here — it's not a coincidence), yet each cooperates with the whole, and each benefits and draws love and strength from that whole. So when that individual goes out into the world, what does he or she find? Other constructs and structures that get people back together.

Let's say a man goes out and gets a job, which usually means that he is working for a company or some other entity that brings people together, but let's jump ahead and say that he works for himself. Then he's not joining a group — or is he? Let's say he found a job selling things on a website. He puts his wares up for sale on the Internet. What happens? He is dependent on people who might want to buy one of his products — another joining together!

Societies and Individuals: The One among the Many

You get the idea. Not only human bodies but also societies were designed with the unity concept in mind. In today's world, you hear a lot about the elevation of the concept of the individual. As much as we agree that each of you is on an individual path, individuals in human societies were meant to be together, like a string of pearls — each pearl beautiful on its own but coming together to form the necklace. Or each of you are a drop of seawater, joining together to make the ocean. How beautiful this concept of "the one among the many" is!

Moving forward, what would it be like if you were not together? If you *were* that one lone individual, what would your life be like? Let's say you are a young woman, you are through with your schooling for the most part, and you're ready to go out into the world and start your life. You move into your own place and you don't have any roommates — you have a place of your own. You're doing fine at first, and you get that job we talked about earlier. But let's say you have a little trouble getting your first job, and it takes several months before you can find one. As an individual you're strong, but you find it a bit lonely. You miss family and friends, and you wish you had someone to talk to. You feel a little less strong, don't you? You are beginning to doubt that being alone will be fun. Why is this? Because people are stronger when they all strive and work together. People support each other, becoming stronger because they are part of a whole.

Opening to Personal Change: The Way Forward

The channel herself [Beverley Bright Star] has been going through a series of these instances, tearing down or doing away with old bad habits and remaking herself into something better. In her heart, she always wanted to make these changes anyway. It's just that we had to *chasten her with love* to get her attention. She took it well and has been making the changes. We knew we needed to do this to get this book out in a timely manner. We had to push her at times, because we feel strongly that this book has a timeliness to it. We want to get the ideas in this book out there because of the urgency of the messages and the times you are in. This book belongs to the masses, and Beverley realized it, stepped up, and made the necessary changes — and the results will be beautiful! So we all know the necessity of character building and integrity building, both within ourselves and within our society as a whole.

Penciling and the Ascension Process

"Penciling" is a term we use when we are talking about how best to put all of the pieces previously mentioned together in a cohesive unit — by *penciling* them together. By this we mean the slow integration, one by one, of each improvement so that in the end all are downloaded and integrated within the original blueprint of each person — not so much the DNA blueprint, but the psychological, emotional, mental, and spiritual blueprints of each person.

Each time something new or revised is brought in, each revision, or rebuild, becomes part of the uniqueness of each person. Thus, it is no longer a rebuild but is *becoming them*, effecting a subtle but full change within each person until, at some point, the ascension process begins and the person achieves their own personal blueprint of perfection. That is where rebuilds and redos eventually lead: to the perfection of each individual as a shining star, returning to the wholeness and unity of the Godhead.Thus we have given a name to a process that goes on all the time with certain people. However, many people are still having trouble with personal change. We want to urge you to get on board and begin striving for that spiritual brass ring. We assure you, it is well worth trying for! As you saw in the bridge storyline, because the construction crew had the humbleness to admit their error, tear the bridge down, and fix it, it became the engineering marvel of the age — and so can you!

4

The Little House in the Woods by the Creek

There once lived a woman named Margery who lived in the woods by a creek. She was a little up there in years but not *old* old. She was just no longer in the full bloom of life. Margery had had a hard life. She had shared this home in the woods with her beloved husband, Dean, who ran a local rock shop in the nearby town. He had been a tinkerer but had also always been fascinated with all different kinds of rocks since he was a boy. The little rock shop that they ran didn't make that much money, but it was just enough to pay the bills, with a little extra left over.

This couple had no children, although they had tried. All they ever had was each other, but that was enough. They had been very happy for many years of marriage, but Dean had died just a year before. Margery had gone through her mourning period, and she had friends who looked in on her from time to time. She was doing fine now, but she missed Dean terribly.

The rock shop Dean had loved so much had closed and been sold a few months earlier. The new store owner had his own ideas about turning it into a little coffee shop or café, so he had called Margery to ask her what he should do with all of the stones. She knew immediately that she wanted them. She didn't know what for, but she knew that she couldn't bear to part with them, because they were part of something that Dean had loved. So she asked the man if he could just pack them up in boxes and bring them over in his truck. He said he wouldn't mind doing that, and they agreed that he would bring them over that weekend.

When the man arrived with all the boxes, Margery asked him to put them on her back porch around the side of the house, and he said he would be glad to. She thanked him, and he arrived that Saturday with a truck half-full of all Dean's rocks and stones to place in the boxes. Margery couldn't wait and tore one of the boxes open. She was rewarded with the sight of gleaming malachite and nuggets of turquoise and tourmaline, a few of which tumbled out on the porch.

"Hmm … I think they like it here," she mused to herself. "Welcome home!" It was getting late, so she picked them up and put them back into the small boxes they had been in. "I'll see you in the morning," she said out loud, and she gave the box a couple of pats.

Very early the next morning, Margery was still lying in bed when she heard a noise out back. She threw on her bed coat and slippers and, rubbing sleep out of her eyes, stood at the back door in wonderment. Her sleek black cat, Margot, had tried to jump up on the tall stack of boxes and missed, knocking a couple of boxes off of the stack. There were stones everywhere, scattered all over that side of the porch. Margery picked up her cat and mockingly scolded her.

"What do you think you're up to?" she cooed. Margot purred and rubbed against Margery's legs as she opened the cupboard to get a can of cat food. "You're such a little brat sometimes, Margot. Really!" She sat down to eat some breakfast and wondered what to do with all the boxes. "Oh well, I'll get to it in a minute," she thought. Now, it just so happened that, once upon a time, Dean had built Margery a garden off to the side and back of the house. He had embedded some smooth river rocks from the creek for a little stepping stone path to the cute little garden gate, with a heart carved out of the middle of the juncture between two bar-room doors. You could open the gate and see grape vines, shrubs, and flowers along with some vegetables. The river-stone path meandered through it, weaving its way around in a large oval until you had walked around the whole perimeter and had seen everything. In the middle stood a large three-tiered fountain, bubbling out a constant flow of water that cascaded down the tiers. It was just a lovely garden! Dean had built it for his wife because she said she wanted one. She missed him so much, especially when she went out in the garden to sit on the squat little bench off to the side of a path where she could see the water from the fountain shining in the sunlight — or the moonlight.

Margery sat at the kitchen table thinking about all of the various colored stones that her husband had collected over the years. Then it occurred to her that it might be nice to put some of them in the garden area, especially the larger stones. So she went out and picked up the mess the cat had created and started pulling boxes down to see if there were any that had larger rocks she could easily put in the garden among the shrubs, vines, and flowers.

She found many larger rocks of varying colors and sizes. She even found some large quartz stones and spent the better part of the day putting them in the garden, careful to place them in just the right spot. "Hmm …" she thought, "the rocks seem to like it here better than being in a box." As she walked through the garden a little later, at dusk, Margery couldn't help noticing how much the rocks had already enhanced the garden. She sat down on the bench and realized that she had just put something that Dean had loved together with something she loved. So, in a way, he was a rock, and she was a garden. And they were together forever!

Margery now had a huge stack of boxes full of the remnants of her husband's life — she realized that these rocks were all she had left of him. Trying not to cry, she took a week or so to slowly and methodically go through all the boxes. She would open them up and see all the different rock collections Dean had. There were so many, and many of them were polished, with shining bands of color from rich dark green to azurite blue. She ended up spreading them out on her whole back porch, putting them into groupings: semiprecious stones over here, quartz crystals of varying colors over there, igneous rocks, marble, and more over there, and so on. Margery was just floored by the number of stones and how varied they were, spread in great array on the back porch. At night she would put several large tarps over them for cover.

One night as she lay in bed, she was staring up at the ceiling thinking about what to do with all of the rocks, when suddenly it came to her. "Oh," she thought, "I could do some artwork with some of them, like rock art. And with some of the others, I could make a stone collage, like a painting outlined and encrusted with different colored stones representing the paint colors and … you know, I could do that. Let me see what I can do tomorrow," she said to herself, brainstorming.

The next day she set to work making this and that, working on all kinds of artistic designs and creations. Ideas just kept coming to her, from little rock figurines to beautifully encrusted stone garden frogs. She even made a unique set of red mushrooms to sit beside the frogs. She also tried her hand at metal work, and at one point she made a life-size statue of a small deer encrusted with beautiful crystals. She even made a snow owl of grey and white quartz with amber eyes. She designed and made a small clay statue with black onyx and green eyes made of real jade that looked just like Margot.

All these projects took months, but Margery was glad to be busy. During this time, she took several art classes to teach herself the latest techniques and methods used in the creation of metal art, pottery, and stonework. Word got out about Margery's work, and people started to come out to see everything she had around the back porch of her little house in the woods by the creek. They did not mind driving that far because, on the porch and indeed in the whole back area, were her art creations. She had been putting some of the best ones in her garden, like the red mushrooms right next to the green frog. "Margot" ended up in the garden too. People from all around would come to see something Margery made, and they would ask her to do one "just like it" for them.

She started getting so many requests that she had to open up a little rock art shop of her own. She kept very busy, and after a while — and the time just flew — ten years had gone by! "Margery's Rock Creations" was very popular, and she found that she enjoyed working with the stones and making them into art pieces. She knew in her heart that Dean was right there encouraging and supporting her, as he had always done. And she silently thanked him every day for inadvertently leaving her a way to discover her own gifts and still be connected to him. It was quite a legacy he had left her! And their love continued on — from a distance, but it continued on. And Margery was content.

And, as fables go, by and by Margery felt herself starting to slip away, as if Dean was pulling her to him. So she sold the shop to some good friends, local artists she had befriended and taught to make her artwork, and settled back in at the little house in the woods by the creek. She passed away soon after, easily and with no suffering. It was a beautiful ending to a beautiful life well lived, and she went to be, at long last, with her beloved Dean.

5

Sacred Journey

There once was a miner name K'alen T'inkatae. He used to dig for gold in the Sudan, but now he was employed as a day laborer at a work camp farther south. This man was a very spiritual man upon the earth. He was not married yet because in his heart he had a mission, some duty that he felt sure that he was supposed to do. However, he was having a lot of trouble figuring out just what that duty would be.

So he drifted from job to job, trying this and that, ever searching for that something that he knew he would feel when he discovered it. Poor K'alen ended up searching for many years, but his prayer had been heard and the desires of his heart would be fulfilled — he just knew it. As the years went by, he even started to try to visualize it, to pull it to himself, and he began to sense that he was very close, very close indeed to materializing it.

Then one day, he met a man who talked about the world, the earth, and life in a way that K'alen had never heard before. And it just so happened to be on chance that K'alen met him. They were both walking along a dirt road in opposite directions. Our K'alen was not lost, per se; he knew where he was generally, but he needed specific directions. So he asked this man walking the other way where such and such was, and the man told him. K'alen thanked him, but as they were starting to walk past each other, the old man said something unusual to him. He said, almost to himself, "I don't think you're going to find what you're looking for there in that village."

K'alen looked back around at him and stopped. "What do you mean, I won't find what I'm looking for?" And the old man said, "I can see that what you are looking for and have been searching your whole life for is not there where you are going. What you are looking for is not a physical place, my son — it is something within you, a spark, a seedling. My son, you do not have to go anywhere — just sit wherever you are, close your eyes, and turn them inward, not outward. There you will find the desire of your heart burning within you."

"How can this be that you know this about me? We've never met before."

"Son" — he was a very old man and K'alen was not young anymore, but this man was even older — "I know we've never met before, but I've had visions of you for many years, so when we were walking along the path, I recognized you immediately. You do not know it yet, but we are not strangers."

K'alen wondered at the man's words but had a feeling of familiarity concerning this man, too. "Why don't we go somewhere and get some supper, and talk a little more?" he asked. The old man agreed, and they walked a mile to the next village and found a small eatery. Just as they were about to sit down, K'alen noticed that the old man didn't seem that old anymore — and he wondered about it.

Meet B'allon

Now our two men had just sat down to have a bite to eat and to talk more. K'alen, bursting with questions but trying to hold back and be calm, said, "First could you tell me, sir, what is your name and where are you from?"

The "old" man paused for a moment and said, "My name is B'allon T'emptae, and I'm from the place you would now call Zimbabwe. My tribe was wiped out a long time ago when I was just a boy. I was able to escape the massacre of my people by slipping out from under a tent and running into the woods. After many days' long journey, I ended up at a friendly village where they took me in and raised me as one of their own. When I was growing up, I was taught many things about the real living world that surrounds us and how to connect with it in a unique way. When I was older, I learned many things that you might call "spiritual technologies" now, and I learned them from different people in our village. You see, everyone in the new village was telepathic and what you would call psychic, but to them it was just normal — everyone there was like that! In their village, that was taken for granted. So here I was, not of their tribe, but they took me in as if I was one of them and treated me as such. And I became one of them."

K'alen replied, "I am very honored to meet you, sir. You had a very interesting upbringing with these unusual people, did you?"

"Yes, I did," said B'allon in reflection. There was a long silence before K'alen ventured on. "So … B'allon, what did you mean when you said that I would not find what I was looking for in the direction that I was headed? What exactly did you mean by that?"

"I just knew that any direction that you were headed for was not going to satisfy you. I could tell and sense that your journey lies inward, son. I could just tell."

"But — you don't even know me. How could you tell something like that just from walking by me? And it was nearly dusk!"

"My son, my son, it is not important now how I could tell. I just could, that's all. But what's important is for me to tell you why I am here, and how I 'know' you. Do not be alarmed, for I was not spying on you. You see, I am what you might call a shaman, and I'm actually much more than that. I am here, K'alen, to show you the way — to guide you to your own path, your own mission in this life. You see, I had a vision of you many years ago. And in this vision, you and I were doing something together, something unusual, something full of mystery and promise. We were working with the energies of the earth and sky. We were dancing on, and in, the rain, creating rainbows and making things green again! And I saw this, my son, many, many years ago. But I knew somehow that we would find a way to meet so that we could begin your training."

K'alen was a bit surprised by the man's words, but he was filled with intense curiosity. Maybe this man could help him to achieve his dream, after all. "My training? What training?"

"Your training to be a person of the sky, my son. For that is what I am. It is what I am called in these parts. In the village that I grew up in, the people were known as the 'people of the sky.' You know," continued B'allon, "in our village we used to look at the stars at night and wonder if anyone else lived 'up there.' Were we the only ones? At least, this is the legend they told me. From long, long ago, many in the tribe often wondered about this. And so one day, as the legend goes, what they thought was a star became very big and bright. Bigger and bigger it got until they saw that something rather large was coming down in front of them right out of the night sky. They were terrified and scattered away, running into their huts. But then a door opened and out stepped a person — she looked human-like — who addressed us, saying in our language, 'We mean you no harm. We are from across the stars and bring you greetings from our world to yours. We are here on a mission of great importance to you and to everyone here on your planet. May we talk with you?'

"The villagers, who had been listening from and peeking out of their huts, slowly stepped out and, feeling quite safe suddenly, welcomed them. The villagers started to kneel, but the new beings said, 'No, no, we are your older brothers and sisters. We are family. We are not gods, but beings like yourselves who have come to make contact with you from our home world, Sirius. We are related to you in a way you cannot understand right now. Please do not worship us, for we are family and are here as friends.'

"And with that, they started a relationship with these star people that lasted over millennia. The star people left and came back many times and taught us many things. They told us of our heritage and of our connection with the stars, and they taught us how to stay connected with them. Sadly, over many years, that knowledge was lost to us, but we still remember many of the things that they taught us. And that's what I am supposed to teach you, my son."

K'alen was quiet for a long time. They got up from the table and embraced. B'allon told K'alen that he had a place to lodge nearby and that K'alen could come and stay with him for a while during the training period. K'alen agreed, and as they were both tired, they retired for the evening. K'alen lay in his bunk thinking of all the amazing and strange but fascinating things B'allon had told him. He looked forward to the next day!

The next morning, B'allon continued with a bit more of his story. "I want you to know, K'alen, that these things that I have to teach you may not be easy at times. There will be times when you may have to trek long distances or up steep mountains to get to the places we will need to go to learn and do our energy work with Mother Earth. Or I may ask you to fast, for example, or to only eat certain things at times in order to awaken your inner sight to the beauty and glories that lie deep within the inner world. Believe me, K'alen, it *is* very beautiful when you look inside yourself and your inner eye opens. You will scarcely be able to believe the adventures that lie within! I will guide you through each step, and we will walk this path together. You will never be alone, for I am and always will be with you now, dear K'alen! For, from my heart to yours, you are now like a son to me, and I will not fail you — *we* will not fail! Now let's begin!" They hugged each other, and set off into the forest.

As they walked along the path, K'alen, who had been silent for quite a while, pondered how quickly his life had changed in just the past twenty-four hours. He felt a deep sense of camaraderie and kinship with this unusual but very good man whom he had met only the afternoon before. He knew that he was putting a lot of trust in this man, but in a strange way he also felt that he had known him for a long time. It was indeed as B'allon had said — there was a deep feeling of recognition that was extremely compelling, but safe. And here he was, all ready to go on this adventure with him even though he hardly knew him, but felt he *did* know him in a larger sense already. And his dream — his mission — was finally starting. How excited he was getting already!

K'alen Begins Training

To his surprise, K'alen's first lesson consisted of going through the forest/jungle and heading up a trail to climb a nearby small mountain. It took them nearly all day to make the journey. B'allon had a machete with him to hack his way through, creating a path for them up the mountain. Fortunately B'allon had also worn a backpack with both water and food provisions for several days. When they reached the summit it was nearly dusk, and they made camp with two small tent-like structures that he had also brought.

As they were setting things up and putting the tents together, K'alen happened to look out on the valley below. As he held up his hand to shield himself from the setting sun, he just happened to look out even farther. In the distance, he could see a tall structure that had been hidden from view on the journey, but now it was barely visible at the top of a mass of encroaching trees and vines of the forest. He could barely make it out, but he thought he saw a star emblazoned onto the upper portion of the pyramid-like structure. He glanced over at B'allon to see if he had seen it, too. B'allon was busy with his head down but looked up at K'alen just then and, looking that way and then back at him, drew a wide grin and just nodded. "We'll get there!" he said.

"Now K'alen, here's what we're going to do. We'll build our small campfire for the night and then I want to show you something."

"Okay." K'alen grinned back.

The sun had just set and the evening twilight had begun. They cleared an area and built a small fire using a flint. Then B'allon went into his tent and came out with something: an unusually shaped rock. It was shaped like a star. Then he led K'alen out to a small cliff nearby and said, "Now we're going to stand here and wait." In a few minutes, as the sun's rays grew less and less, there was a star that started twinkling low on the horizon. And it was twinkling directly over the pyramid-like structure across the valley. All of a sudden, both men saw the star that had been barely visible to them earlier light up a bit, catching both the star's early light and the last of the sun's fading rays. "Look!" B'allon shouted, and the star-shaped rock in his hand started blinking and twinkling also! K'alen could hardly believe his eyes and rubbed them a little. He was incredulous and speechless — it was really quite a sight! Holding for only a few minutes as the sunlight faded and nighttime was fully upon them, they looked at each other in wonder and awe.

They sat by the fire and talked until late, talking of many things and getting to know each other more. K'alen told B'allon of his life and his many jobs and journeys. He told him of the singular dream that pursued him, always leaving him feeling unfulfilled and restless. He related how his grandmother had told him that someday, far into the future, he would find his way and his dream, and that he should never stop looking for it and never give up hope. It had warmed his heart to know that at least one person in his life understood him and his dreams. "Do not ever give up on finding your dream," she had said, "but more than that, do not ever give up on yourself,

K'alen! You are a fine young man and deserve to find whatever it is that your heart yearns for, hungers for. I know for certain in my own heart that you will succeed someday. I feel it — I know it!" And that was the last time he ever saw her, but he had carried her words in his heart all these years. "Don't ever give up on yourself!" she had said. And he never did!

Introduction to Meditation

Now, they had just seen the marvelous star form on the pyramid-like structure across the way. B'allon had pressed hard that day because he wanted K'alen to see it right at dusk, as it was a portent of what was to come for him. The star had represented itself three times that night. It represented the two men and a star showing the way, the way of the inner star making its first fiery appearance in K'alen's life. As a shaman in training, he mystically connected to it and what it now represented in his life: his new beginning.

B'allon and K'alen got up the next morning, packed, and went back down the small mountain toward the pyramid. When they arrived later that afternoon, the sun was shining bright and hot above them, and the heat was oppressive. As they approached the structure, they could see what appeared very intricately carvings in great detail on the side of the pyramid. B'allon only let K'alen look at a few of them before he indicated that they needed to get to the top of the pyramid by sundown. So up they both continued until they reached the top of it. Again, what a sight it was that greeted them as they looked out over the valley to the mountain they had been on the night before! K'alen was already wishing they had stayed there one more night, but B'allon had other plans. "We will go back again someday," he said.

As the sun set behind the mountain, both men saw again the twilight star, twinkling and almost beckoning to the two of them as they stood atop the pyramid. K'alen, looking below his feet over the side, saw the giant star catch the light as before, only this time it looked almost translucent, like a thousand shimmering diamonds in the fading light. "Close your eyes," said B'allon softly. "Close your eyes, and tell me what you see." K'alen did so. He could no longer see the glistening diamonds under his feet, but he could feel them in a sense. His inner sight remained dark, however.

"I don't see anything, but I can feel the presence of the star below our feet. Could we sit down on the top of this for a while?"

"Yes, my son, that's a good idea. Why don't we both sit?"

They moved a little away from the edge and got seated in a comfortable position. K'alen immediately closed his eyes and sat for a while. Again, he did not "see" anything, but the presence and warm glow of the crystals continued to bring him comfort. His mind seemed to be drawn inward. Deeper and deeper his mind went until he felt as if he was being held in suspended animation, he was so deep. At one point, he thought he saw a tiny pinpoint of soft blue light floating in the middle of his inner vision. Curious, he would move toward it, but it remained elusive. After a while, he started coming back up and out of the trance, and he realized he didn't know how long they had been sitting there. He thought it had been just a few minutes — maybe a half-hour or forty-five minutes. He opened his eyes to see that B'allon was no longer seated next to him.

K'alen heard some rustling not too far away and looked around to see B'allon back over to his left sitting wrapped in a small blanket. "How long was I sitting there?" B'allon replied, "You've been sitting there for three hours, my son. Night is now upon us."

K'alen was dumbfounded! "You mean I … I was sitting there with my eyes closed for three hours? Are you serious?"

"I am totally serious, my son. You didn't realize it, but you went into a deep meditative state quickly and stayed there for most of the time. I've never seen anyone go as deep as you that fast. You're quite a natural at this, I'll tell you that much!"

"I'm quite a natural at what?" K'alen demanded.

"Why, at meditating! That is what we were doing."

"Oh, I didn't know that's what it was. It just felt good to do it, that's all."

"Yes, yes. Did you see or sense anything?" B'allon wanted to know.

"Yes. At first I felt like the rocks were, in a way, communicating something to me, and their help felt comforting. And then I guess that's when I lost track of time. But at some point, I saw a tiny blue and gold light with a star in it floating around at what looked like a far distance at first, then closer at other times. Then I lost track of it and came out of the 'meditation' — is that what you call it?"

"Yes, that's what you call it. Let's get some sleep right now since it is now late, and we'll talk in the morning, okay?"

"Okay, that's fine. I'm pretty tired anyway." They bedded down for the night, and K'alen fell into one of the deepest sleeps that he had ever had.

Unanswered Questions

K'alen had just had his first experience with meditation, and it was a profound one. He found out that he was good at this new, very unusual way of seeing and doing. He was not sure if he *did* anything exactly, and he asked B'allon to explain the next morning as they were eating their sparse morning meal. He had many questions. "What happened? Why did I lose track of time? What was the blue dot? Why did I feel the crystals? Were they talking to me? And what was that odd, but good, feeling in my head and body?"

"Whoa, whoa — one at a time, please!" interrupted B'allon, laughing. He shook his head. "Let's finish eating and I will answer every one of your questions as we continue on our journey today. For we have one more place we must go, and it is a long way. So let's get going and climb down off of the pyramid. Let's get well on our way, and then we can talk, okay?"

K'alen nodded his assent. He was so very excited to hear the answers, though, that he too hoped they would get going fast. He was very impatient at the same time, however, because of how many years he had waited, and now he had to wait a few more hours. But K'alen was beginning to learn to be patient with B'allon, and that in his own time he would give him the answers — and more.

Connecting with the Stones

So on they battled, carefully climbing down and through the thick vines and vegetation that surrounded the pyramid. Once they were down and well on the path, B'allon found his voice. "Well, my boy, to answer one of your questions is to answer all of them. Remember back to last night, when we were both standing very near the edge of the top of the pyramid? I had us both stand there that close so that you could be aware of and peek over the edge to see the dazzling display of the crystals embedded in the stones of the upper part of the pyramid. You see, my son K'alen, we — the people of the sky — built that pyramid a long time ago with the help of the star people, and they taught us how to construct it and where to find stones that would be as a beacon to them each time they came back to visit. They wanted there to be a special place, the same place, every time they came. We would get the signal that they were on their way, and then send a contingency from our village to go meet them there and bring them back to our village. And there is one more thing that I have not told you about yet. We will get to that in a bit."

K'alen listened raptly as they were walking along and hacking through the jungle. His eyes were a little heavy, though, and his ears were burning slightly, but they kept walking. B'allon continued. "Now remember that we closed our eyes briefly, and then we stepped back from the edge to continue our meditation. You closed your eyes again and felt the stones, didn't you?"

"Yes, I did actually. Why was that?"

"Well, it was because they, the stones, were connecting with you; they were talking to you, and although I know you didn't hear it yet, they were singing you a song, because I heard them, too! They were acknowledging your presence, K'alen, because they can tell when someone is there they can communicate with. They sang you a song of greeting, from their souls to yours, welcoming you and starting what will be a lifelong relationship with you, K'alen. From now on, you do not have to be near them. Just picture them in your mind and you will be instantly and intimately connected, anytime, anywhere!"

K'alen stopped on the path for a second. "Wait, B'allon," he said. "Seriously? For real?"

"For real." They resumed walking along the path.

The People of the Sky

"Okay, so then …" K'alen was speaking slowly now, trying to take all this in at once. He was almost afraid to ask the next question, one that he had asked earlier that day. "So then, if the rock crystals were singing and communicating with me and welcoming me, then … what happened while I was sitting there for three hours, as you said? What was going on there?" His voice lilted a bit asking the question.

"Well, you see, they — we — constructed the pyramid in a certain way so that when you sit more towards the center on the top, you are better able to connect with the star people's emanations, and it makes it easier to communicate with them. As I said before, you are to become one of us now — you are now one of the people of the sky, and it is my mission and privilege to teach you the old ways of our people and their connection with all things on our planet, my son," said B'allon, very solemnly and very slowly. "Come — let us make camp for the night, as we have another full day's journey tomorrow."

And they made camp, hardly eating or speaking for the rest of the evening. K'alen went off by himself for a while. He was overwhelmed by the stupendous news and the incredible honor just bestowed on him. He could scarcely take it all in. Even when he lay down for the night, he lay there for a long time just looking up at the stars and wondering. He felt humbled and honored by his sudden change of fortune. Whatever benevolent being or force that had brought the two of them to that first meeting must have been very wise, indeed. The synchronicity of it was mind-boggling, to say the least!

The insects flying around his head finally settled down, and he fell into a very deep sleep. All of a sudden he found himself running, running, running with a herd of antelope. In his dream state he was easily able to keep up with them as he ran, leaped, and jumped with the best of them. Suddenly, he was in the middle of a large herd of wild elephants, running alongside them, laughing and playing with them. They trumpeted his name and he trumpeted back to them as if he were one of them. Then he found himself in the middle of a group of wild hogs, running and grunting with them in search of food. They looked over at him and snorted a funny welcome. The next thing he knew, he catapulted over a large hedge right into the middle of a pride of lions. He lay very still as one of the larger ones, a very old one with an extremely large head and mane, walked slowly over to him and smelled him. His heart was racing a mile a minute! The great lion spoke (not audibly, but in K'alen's head): "I see you are now one of us. You are one of the star people's messengers, sent here as of old. My memory grows dim and I am the last and only one who remembers the old ways — the old days when Man and Beast spoke together and lived together as one, in respect and service to each other. I recognized your energy and vibration, and you have nothing to fear from us, for we are your solemn and good friends upon this earth. You are always welcome, my son."

Then immediately K'alen felt a very strong pulling sensation, and he was pulled back out of the dream very suddenly. He lay there awake for a while. The dawn was just beginning to break, and there were a few stars left. "That dream felt so real," he thought. "I should remember to ask B'allon about it." And he drifted back asleep for a few more hours.

An Extraordinary Dream

Now we know that K'alen has begun learning to meditate and is just beginning his journey to the inner realms. He is filled with awe at the beautiful new world that is opening up to him, a world he never even dreamed was there.

B'allon stirred from his sleep the night before and looked over to where K'alen was sleeping, but he was not there. He glanced around and spied him sitting a little distance away. K'alen had his eyes closed and had been sitting in meditation for about a half-hour. He heard B'allon stir and get up, but he was by that time so engrossed and inwardly focused that it seemed as if B'allon was far away. K'alen was breathing very slowly and rhythmically, as B'allon had shown him that night on the pyramid. He "went away" for a short while inside his head/mind but would get pulled back by random thoughts. Back and forth he went until it seemed time to open his eyes. B'allon was sitting there quietly beside him and just smiled at him. They quickly ate breakfast, and K'alen, knowing not to ask B'allon questions until they were on the trail, waited patiently for the questions and answers to begin.

They had been on the trail for about a half-hour when B'allon turned around and said, "So, you had quite an interesting dream last night, didn't you, K'alen?" he said. K'alen replied, "How did you know? Yes, I did, actually. I dreamed that I was running with different herds of animals, and that not only was I able to keep up with them, but I could talk to them, too! And they would answer back to me as if I was one of them! One time I was a wild hog running around searching for food. It's as if I can still smell the musty earth as we rooted in it looking for tender roots and vegetables. Before that I was running and playing with the elephants. They seemed to love me as one of their family. We all trumpeted back and forth in the gayest manner, nuzzling each other's trunks and playing hide-and-go-seek. What fun that was! Oh, and I ran and ran with the antelope people. I felt as one with them, too, and felt like I could run forever. We sprang over rocks and small streams — it was wonderful to run so fast and not get tired!" B'allon cut in on this dialogue, asking what was it about the dream experience that he liked the most. K'alen replied, "I loved how real it felt — it did not *feel* like a dream at all."

Then B'allon said, "Now, K'alen, go back into your mind now, back into the dream. Are you doing that now?"

"Yes, yes — it's like I am right there again."

"Okay, now this time, rise above the scene and watch it from above or the side, and try to see yourself. Can you try that?"

"Okay, yes ... okay ... there — there I am. I'm running with the antelope herd, but I'm having a hard time seeing myself because ... oh, I think I *am* an antelope, too, in the dream! I did not realize that when I was in the dream that I had become one of them. Let me try that with the other ones, too. Okay ... okay, there I am — I'm a baby elephant running with my mother and the herd. Oh, how fun! Okay, now ... oh, ugh! I'm a hog, too, just like one of them, but it's not so fun with your nose in the dirt all the time. *Eeugh* — yuck! All right then, let me quickly check the last part of my dream. Oh, no, it's kind of fading back now. I'm having trouble remembering that part ..."

B'allon just laughed and kept walking. "Don't worry, K'alen. When you are ready, it will come back to you. Now let's stop for lunch. This is really pretty right here, and we have time to stop to eat. Let's take a little rest." And they ate and talked some more about dreams in general, and the different meanings of different dreams.

Some dreams were just regular dreams, nonsensical much of the time; but then some dreams, like K'alen's, were much more than ordinary.

"You see, K'alen, the kind of dream you had is called a 'lucid dream,' where you feel as if you are in the dream itself. I know you don't know how to do this yet, but you will get to the point where you can consciously drive the action of the dream and control it to a large extent. You can even wake yourself up if you like, or stay in longer for more pleasant dreams. These are the kinds of things that I can teach you how to do. You can even have mental telepathy with the 'dream movers,' as we call them. The star people taught us that, my son. They taught us that and many other things, like how we are related to them."

"And how *are* we related to them, B'allon? How can that be?"

"My son, I do not know for sure how, for the villagers rarely talked about that, but we were taught that long ago, so long ago that no one remembers how long, they had come and left some of their numbers, their people, here on our planet to help us along our evolutionary path. Again, this was said to have occurred far, far back in the past. Now even we had trouble believing this, but they had never lied to us, so we believed that it must have been true. Where or exactly when, nobody knew, but we certainly did look a lot like them in many ways. Our skin color, of course, was much darker and our hair was different, but in most other respects, we were very much alike. We were more alike than different, I will say that!"

K'alen pondered this for a while as they got on their way. They did not say anything for a long while, each in their own thoughts. The sun made its way across the sky, and clouds began to form quickly from behind a nearby cliff. They were heading towards it when, just as quickly as they had formed, the clouds let loose with a downpour. K'alen and B'allon ran for the cliff overhang, but it was still a quarter mile away, and they were drenched by the time they found shelter under the large overhanging rock. They laughed and laughed, but exclaimed how good the rain felt after so much heat day after day.

"Let's make camp early today!" B'allon shouted over the still-pouring rain.

"Okay!" K'alen shouted back. "No problem! I think that's a very good idea!"

And with that they settled in and made a small camping area where it was still dry.

The moon came up very bright later that evening after the clouds had cleared, as they were sitting in meditation. It was just a lovely, balmy night in the jungle. They slept well.

The Next Morning

"How did you sleep?" K'alen asked the next morning.

"Oh , I slept very well, thank you. I always do, K'alen, my son. I always do."

They got under way very early on this morning. The night sounds of the animals and insects had not quite died down yet when they left their dry area for the thick jungle again. This day, though, would be different, for this would be the day that K'alen would remember for the rest of his life. Today they would meet the shamans that B'allon had trained under. K'alen did not know it, but they were headed toward B'allon's village where he had grown up.

The village itself was not remarkable looking in any way. It looked like a traditional African village of its time. There were, however, two men guarding the way into it, and they were cordial but friendly. They recognized B'allon immediately and welcomed him with open arms. B'allon introduced K'alen and told them that he was there to live with them for a while in order to learn the old ways of their people before the knowledge was lost forever. Each one of the villagers approached K'alen, took his hand, smiled, and said, "Welcome." One by one they all came up to greet him and invite him to supper. His heart swelled with emotion to think that just a few days before, he had had no family and knew no one, and now he had both family and friends! His dream had already led him this far, and he was content.

He stayed and lived in the village. He became one of them and learned the mystical ways of the villagers. B'allon adopted him and taught him everything he knew. And when B'allon died, it was said that he had lived to be 390 years old. He was buried with his ancestors on a nearby hill. K'alen wept when he died. He put the star-rock on top of his grave as a tribute and a symbol of gratitude for what B'allon had given him on that summer night so very long ago.

K'alen became famous far and wide for his keen abilities and good heart. He married and had ten children, twelve grandchildren, and thirty-five great grandchildren and lived a long, happy, and productive life. His dream had not only been realized — it had been filled to overflowing. And all of this happened over 5,000 years ago!

Analysis and Overview

Now let's get back to our story about the two men in ancient Africa. And now that you know that this story was not set in modern times, what did you think, dear reader? Would you like to have some fun and go back through a few points in the story? Okay, then.

Remembering that this story is a fable and we can do this just because we can, let's treat this as if it is a modern-day story, shall we? So we have

K'alen, who we know has traveled all around working at different jobs, hasn't he? But in prehistoric Africa, what kind of jobs might he have been doing? In our present day you might have envisioned him almost as an indigent person, going from work camp to work camp doing nothing but menial jobs, having to live in the bad parts of towns, and so on. But here we have K'alen who, now that we know, could have been working in an ancient gold mine. We know from ancient records that these existed perhaps much further back than 5,000 years ago. So if we transport ourselves back to that time, then we will envision K'alen not as a poor itinerate worker, but as someone of substance and character, a high-minded individual who is indeed making his way around much of the continent working as, say, a highly skilled laborer, or as an escort to a sultan's caravan. Or perhaps he visited ancient Egypt at the time of the pharaohs.

Who Was K'alen?

There are many possibilities of who exactly K'alen was and what his "walkabout" could have been about. We are not sure, and in the end it doesn't matter, does it? Because we each see a part of ourselves in him, don't we? We can relate so vividly to his search for something he has trouble explaining to others but feels so keenly inside. And we can all relate to the chance meeting, the hitherto unknown synchronistic quality of that meeting, and the pivoting of his life around it. And we realize and can relate to his ever-changing inner panorama — his suddenly rich, active, and profoundly satisfying inner life that informed the whole rest of his life. These are the kinds of things that we all can relate to.

We are touched when, for the first time in his life, K'alen has a real family. We are touched when he sees and feels the crystals come alive and sing to him. And we are with him when he realizes, for perhaps the first time, that all are family, that all are one, that all have the same heart, the same soul, the same spark of life, the same perfection designed by the Infinite. He felt, as we do, that we are all in this world together. That, like the stones, we can all care about and support each other, help each other, love each other — that we all share a common experience. And that experience is called life.

As we were following him around in the story, did you notice, dear reader, that he would go through a mental process that "advanced"? Doubtful and highly skeptical at first, he was able to grasp and accept a lot of new concepts and situations quite rapidly and astutely. Did you notice that he was already able to connect both his head and his heart? He adeptly and smoothly assessed and processed some very complex situations in a highly efficient manner. To say it the way we do nowadays, a lot was thrown at him all at once. And he handled it well, did he not? We give him plenty of kudos on that one — he gets an A. In trusting his feelings but making sure to check with his head: an A+. And for having an open mind to allow all of this to occur and not cop an attitude: A++!

So you are beginning to see that our friend K'alen had a lot going for him even at the get-go, didn't he? So we would probably say now that he was ready. He was more than ready for this experience. He caught the fly ball, didn't he? He not only caught it, but he jumped very high and literally pulled it out of the air to himself, didn't he? A magnificent leap into the air to catch it that takes your breath away, doesn't it? Whew! We are so proud of him!

And what about B'allon? If this had been in modern times, what would we perceive about him? Who was he, really? Watching the story in modern times, one might be afraid, especially at first, that the old man was a crackpot or looking to steal from poor K'alen when they were sleeping. We wouldn't know at first if we could trust him, would we? But looking at it from the perspective that we have now, what can we draw from the facts that were given? He was raised by an apparently very old prehistoric tribe of people who had connections with a race from another planet, another solar system — possibly a sister planet. In the story, we stated that this happened over 5,000 years ago, but what if it was more like 50,000 years ago? This is a fable, right? And what if the people of that day and time period of Earth's history were indeed able to live for hundreds of years? And what if, indeed, their whole village was really more full of the star people than not? What if?

You see the endless possibilities here, do you not? Our B'allon could have been one of the original star people, so then perhaps he was handing the proverbial keys of the kingdom to our K'alen, to put it another way. Learning to meditate from a master, having your dreams interpreted by an expert, and so on — those possibilities do exist. They are and can be inherent in the story if you look deeply enough and see the layers upon layers upon multilayers. It gets very exciting and mind provoking, doesn't it?

From such a simple story to one that you want to re-read again and again so that you can pay more attention to all the details that, in retrospect, make you want to go back over it, don't they?

Put Yourself in the Story

Now we're going to do something new here. We're going to have you, the reader, be interactive in the story. It will be a little like the 1950s instructional mini-movies known as the *You Are There* series. Let's have you walk along in front of K'alen as he is following B'allon on that first morning when they start the hike through the jungle. And as we are walking with him, we see that he is happy but still a bit apprehensive. So, as they hack their way through the thick jungle, they come to a place on the path that turns ever so slightly in another direction. B'allon knows where he is going, but we do not — not yet!

So we're going to be walking along in between the two men on the trail. Now, what K'alen doesn't know is what B'allon is doing, but *we* see — and we see it because we are walking along but also watching both of them as if we were watching a movie. B'allon is able to read K'alen's thoughts, and so we see this happening from a view over the action, looking down. From this vantage point, we can see far ahead on the path that B'allon is creating and we can also see way, way behind K'alen. Neither man knows we are there, of course, as we are inserting ourselves unseen after the fact, aren't we? And we are rising above the path so that we can have a better view of the action. So, as they are walking along, we see that B'allon is already aware of what K'alen is going through, how he is processing the start of his new life with B'allon. B'allon just smiles to himself, as he knows that he has to give K'alen the time he needs to think things through.

Okay, so here's what B'allon is seeing (only about six to ten feet in front of him, if that, due to the thickness of the jungle), and here is what K'alen is seeing, because he is so deep in thought that he's not really looking. And when he looks, he sees B'allon on the trail a little further ahead. Basically he only sees B'allon ahead of him, and that's all. So, both men are walking in the present moment, and they are seeing the future ahead of them on the path — and the past behind them. But here's the thing : *We* see it all! From our vantage point slightly above, we can see B'allon walking — the present moment, and the path ahead of him — the immediate future — and K'alen behind him — his immediate past. From our point above, then, we can see past, present, and future all at the same time — all at once — as if all of it was happening at the same precise moment! Now, can you grasp this, dear reader? Because we are not really talking about the two men on the path anymore, are we? Now we are starting a dialogue about the nature of time itself. Is there truly a past and a future — or is there only the present?

As you can see from our illustration of the *You Are There* phenomenon, it is indeed possible that they are all happening together. We know this is a bit mind-boggling, but we are hoping to get you to understand that you can be in the present moment, but be aware of the fact — or at least be willing to open your mind and concede to the fact — that this could be a concrete possibility. Could this be true that time itself does not exist as we think it does, in a linear fashion, but in a quantum state — the ever-present *present*? Can you fathom this, dear reader? Can you open your mind a little at least, and think about the possibility of it? We invite you to do just that. And if you say, "No, no, that could just not be possible," then we invite you to put yourself back into the story with K'alen and B'allon on the path, with us overhead. Keep looking at that from that other perspective — the larger view from above — and keep thinking about it. Take your time and let yourself process it back and forth, and see what you come up with, okay?

All right, dear reader, have you had time to think about what we discussed? Have you been able to "fly over the top" of the scene in the jungle to see more of the overview? If you are ready, we want to expand that vision a bit and — are you ready? — apply it to your view of how the whole world operates in this third-dimensional realm.

How Time Really Operates

Einstein's theory of relativity and his idea of how time operates were blockbusting at the time, but we are extending you forward from that point, so let's use it as a basis, shall we?

In his theories, he stated that time was a bit like a ribbon, ebbing and flowing like a wave of finely tuned macro-time filaments of light that wave and bend, ending up almost like a circle of concentric waves, looping out and out upon each other, ad infinitum.

Now we want you to consider, too, dear reader, that the passage of time really is not a "passage"; it is merely a stringing together of moment on moment on moment. But it is not linear, really, at all. In your third-dimensional mind, it seems as though one moment precedes another moment and so on — or so it would seem. But we beg you to consider that it only appears that way. Now, we realize that this is a powerful illusion, to be sure. But try to wrap your mind around the fact that just because it seems like something is so doesn't mean it really is. In the larger universe of which you are all a part, there are fluctuations and events that go on all the time that your scientists have always had trouble explaining. They have this theory and that theory, and they try to make it work. And we love our scientists — they are working hard to explain the phenomenon of these things and of the perplexities of time itself.

Time: A Quantum Reality

What we are trying to do here is to ask you, dear readers, to realize that your physical bodies and the physical third-dimensional universe itself do not just operate on a 3D level; the universe and your bodies exist and operate in many different dimensions simultaneously! "How can that be?" we hear you say as you read this. "How can we be here, in the third dimension, and be there in the fourth or fifth dimension at the same time?" Remember, dear readers how, when you look out at the stars, you realize that you are seeing light that is coming to your eyes from the past — in fact, the very distant past, do you not? And you do not realize it, but the light itself is interdimensional. It bends and flows on its way to your eyes through space and time like an interdimensional ribbon to arrive at the point where your eyes can detect and see it.

Life-trons and the Body of Light

I think most of you realize by now that your body consists of light and something called "life-trons," a word coined and used by Paramahansa Yogananda in his famous book *Autobiography of a Yogi*. In the book, life-trons are what scientists now refer to as the space in between the atoms. Within this space is where the life-trons and the light reside. And since we just indicated that light has an interdimensional quality to it, your three-dimensional body is really much more than that, is it not? So if it is physical matter — three-dimensional — with interdimensionality in between and also intertwining within the DNA itself, then your body is actually multidimensional, too! So it appears to be only three-dimensional but, in truth, exists in more than one dimension at the same time. And accepting that, then, we will move on — or are we moving back? — to our original statement regarding an expanded definition of time and how our physical bodies lie within that framework. It seems one way, but the fabric of the reality itself is really much, much more than most people realize.

And so, dear readers, we have given you much to think about, have we not? We will touch on it again later in the book. So please, have fun thinking about and discussing this one, and do pick up a copy of Paramahansa Yogananda's book, *Autobiography of a Yogi*, and check on chapter 43 there too. It will greatly enhance and further explain points we have made here.

The Soup and the Arrow

We just discussed the nature and fabric of time. Are you now better able to discern for yourselves, dear readers, how time moves more in a circle, a bit like soup in a pan? Now this is not to say that it is exactly a "linear" soup going round and round, because it is not, but it is much like an arrow that is flying. The front of the arrow is, at first glance, ahead of the back of the arrow, but they both arrive at the destination at the same time. So if we combine the two — the circular past-present-future soup with the front (future)-center (present)-back (past) arrow, you could say that technically they are all happening and arriving at the same time!

Psychics: Interpretation Is Key

This is what psychics "see" when they give you a prediction of a future event. They sense, see, and feel the future but have to interpret what they feel correctly. Often it helps the psychic to have experience interpreting what it feels like for them. If they sense a five, does this mean five weeks, five years, or some other time frame? Doing it many times helps the accuracy of the interpretation because the psychics are seeing the future event happening in their now moment of seeing it. And here's the kicker: They can only see it as it is connected to the possibilities and probabilities from that exact moment that they are asked to look!

If, say, you are Edgar Cayce or Nostradamus, and you are able to see the arrow, then you realize that the front of the arrow, the future, is attached to the middle of the arrow, the present. So, if the arrow that is red all of a sudden is green, then the red future event will now be green. Do you see, dear readers? If you are Nostradamus and you see the future, you know and would admit that because the future is informed by the present moment, if that present moment totally changes, then the future is and will be totally changed too!

We want to give you another illustration. In the movie *Back to the Future II*, the present moment changed when old Biff went back, obtained the sports almanac, came back, and gave it to young Biff, who changed *that* present moment by using the almanac. It changed the future, did it not? That would be another example of how the present directly affects the future. Do you see, dear readers?

A Changed Future from a Changed Present

So if you were Nostradamus and you looked from your time in the fourteenth century forward, you would see destruction and cataclysms happening in Earth's future *if nothing came along to drastically alter it*! But then, what if Nostradamus were alive in the 1970s, and enough people around Earth started to make positive, heart-filled changes in their lives — then what would he have predicted from that point in time in Earth's history? Would he still have made the predictions that he did about our future, or would he have been able to give us a better outlook because, you see, his starting point would then have been very different, would it not?

In fact, the accuracy of many of the dire predictions from past psychics such as Nostradamus and Edgar Cayce has dropped off severely, hasn't it? In fact most, if not all, of the "end of the world" predictions did not happen, nor will they. The answer is obvious: We are all still here! The comet didn't have to strike us; the massive, continent-sinking earthquakes did not have to happen, because you changed! We congratulate you all for having the courage to make those changes and do the work when you did it! It takes at least 51 percent of the world population to effect that large of a change, but a changed *present* informed a changed *future!*

Now you are beginning to understand the operation of how time is not so much linear as it is a view overlooking a path, or soup swirling in a pot, or the back-center-front arrow. These are different ways of seeing that, as incredible and unbelievable as this concept is, time is not really linear; it only seems to be. We want you to open your mind and think about these illustrations and these points for yourself.

So, now you understand a little better why 2012 is only going to be the end of an age or the end of the world, as explained so eloquently in Gregg Braden's book *Fractal Time*, published a few years ago. Read his book, and we think you will all start to think differently about time!

What Was Real

B'allon also taught K'alen how to anchor cosmic energy in the sacred energy grid of the planet at that time. Now this story is actually not a made-up story; this one really happened! K'alen and B'allon were not their real names, but this is a true story and actually did happen. Everything in the story is real, especially the connection with the people of the stars (sky). They came to the Dogon tribe, B'allon's adopted tribe (which was originally from Vega) to give the indigenous peoples of the world at that time the ability to help maintain the energy grids of Earth. They actually taught them many other advanced healing techniques and how to do advanced energy work from Sirius to help Earth become the beautiful Eden that it did.

The reason that we tell this to you, our readers, is to reach out to you from our star system, Sirius, and give the people of Earth our blueprint for the new age — a gift from all of us to all of you. The parables and teachings included in this book are a primary look at the moral code of the law of one that the people of Sirius think you, the people of Earth, are ready for, need, and have earned. This is your next step — the (new) Age of Aquarius is upon you!

Use the peaceful and loving energies that this time is bringing in to your full advantage. This book, among others, will help to clarify many things and get you all started on the road to becoming the galactic humans we already know you are becoming. Use this as a reference book and workbook to learn these principles well, and apply them in your daily lives. We know that there are so many misconceptions and confusing and erroneous beliefs floating around on Earth, and we feel that addressing these issues across the board might just clarify and catalog some of these issues for everyone here.

We have put this information in a parable format with animals as the "stars" of the stories to avoid any of the prejudice, grandstanding, or finger pointing that we know some people do. We wanted to avoid and bypass all of that to be able to concentrate on the interlayering of the lessons in each story. Paramahansa Yogananda, that great guru and mystic from the East, used animal parables — very amusingly so, at times — in his stories on the meditation techniques and secrets of the great yogis of India to great effect. We have framed our stories in a similar fashion, only ours are much, much more intricate, embedded, and interlayered.

This is our gift — from Lily, the Syrian Council of 12, and the hearts of all of the people of Sirius to the hearts of all of you. Enjoy.

6

Charles

Charles was a rambunctious young ram who loved to go prancing around every morning, just for the joy of it. He loved running around in the fields, kicking up his heels, and running up all the hills. He was always the first one out of his enclosure because he hated feeling constricted and fenced in. Even when it was extremely cold and he should have stayed under cover, he would be a rascal and break out of the enclosure to go running. He just could not help himself — he had such an ebullient spirit!

His mother could not get him to listen to her. "Now, Charles, it is very cold and it is snowing. You should stay here with us for shelter. We all keep each other warm. Why won't you stay?"

"But Maaa-maaa," he would bleat, "the field is calling to me, Maaa-maaa. I might miss something out there. Please?" And with that he would head-butt the gate a couple of times. Charles was a small ram, but he had a strong neck and little horns already appearing. Next thing his mother knew, out he'd go — lickety split — to run to his favorite field. He didn't get very far this day, however, and he slipped and fell into the mud. But he got up and got going again, running to his favorite hill that he was so fond of looking out at. Then he slipped again! This didn't seem to faze him, though. He struggled to his feet and clambered on up. "I just have to get to my lookout point. I need to see the big sky!" he cried to himself. "Then I'll go back in. It *is* pretty cold today."

He laboriously reached the top of a small hill, and there it was! It was such a beautiful vista, even blanketed by the near blizzard of this particular day. "Look at this," said Charles. "Look at how beautiful the world is today! I don't care if it is snowing. I just have to see it every day!"

The snowflakes started piling up on top of his nose and his eyelashes had little flakes on them. He shook them off and saw his warm breath streaming in the frigid air. "Okay, now I've seen it. Mama was right — I'd better get on home now," he thought.

So just as fast as he had come, our little ram slipped and slid all the way down the hill, but he didn't care. He'd seen the *scene* — he'd made it to the top of the great hill and had seen the world!

He stumbled clumsily, thoroughly elated, and ran back under the cover of the enclosure, shivering but happy. His mother patiently licked all the snow off him and just looked at him. She just did not know what to do with this boy — he was so impetuous! But he seemed fine every time he did it. He always came back safe and sound, so she had learned not to worry so much.

"Oh, Charles." She sighed in her motherly ewe way. "You are such a stubborn-headed little ram!"

"Don't be mad at me, Maaa-maaa," he would reply contritely. "I just can't help it — I have to see the sky! I have to make sure that it is still out there every day, Maaa-maaa. Don't you see?" he pleaded.

"The sky? Why, son, the sky is always there, it's just ... sometimes it is blue and sometimes it is gray with fluffy things in it, but it's always there. And it's always going to be there, honey. Don't worry! In my whole life, every time I woke up, there was the sky. That's all I can tell you, honey — you don't have to worry. It will always be there — just in different colors, that's all."

Charles listened to his mother. He thought about what she said, but that wasn't enough. "Are you sure, Maaa-maaa? Are you sure it's going to be there every day? 'Cause I just have to know! I just have to run up the hill and see it so wide and so beautiful for myself, Maaa-maaa! That's why I have to run so hard every day, don't you see?"

She shook her head and replied, "No, honey, I don't know why you can't just accept what I'm telling you. I've got more experience than you, and I've been around a long time. I've never seen it go away or not be there in the morning when we wake up."

Charles blinked his eyes. "Yes, I hear you, Maaa-maaa, but I just have to see it with my own eyes. Don't you see? I have to know for myself that it is real. Don't you see that, Maaa-maaa?"

"Yes, honey, I think I'm beginning to see that you need to find out for yourself. Just please keep yourself safe and come back, okay? Mama can't help but worry!"

"Okay, Maaa-maaa. I will," Charles bleated. And he nestled his head against his mother and fell asleep.

So every morning, our young ram Charles would be first out of the starting gate — *whoosh*, off he'd go — like a shot! He would run straight to the hill, "the great hill," as he called it, to make sure that the sky was there. You see, as a young ram, he was never sure that it was going to be there, even though his mother had said it always would be. No, he had to confirm it for himself. He just felt like something was not right with the world — his world — until he made contact with the sky. And the view! He felt so connected with the world from his little hill that each time he saw the view, he was content.

One particular day, as usual, Charles was the first one out of the enclosure and went running up his hill. He stood there, feasting his eyes on everything he could see from there: the clouds billowing, forming, and reforming in their march across the sky; the green grass on a far hill; an "emerald-in-the-sun" mountain in the distance; and over on the north side, the deep-blue vastness of the ocean off in the distance, catching the sun, glistening, and shimmering its way back to his eagerly watching eyes. He took a deep breath and said to himself, "Here it is. Here it is. It's the whole world, and I can see it for myself. And the sky is still here, and I'm part of it. I'm part of it too!"

Suddenly, he heard a voice from the sky: "Charles! Charles, can you hear me?" It was a deep rumbling voice, like thunder, only it was not frightening at all. It was a deep, soothing, fatherly voice.

"I can hear you. Who are you?" Charles replied.

"I am the voice of All That Is, my son."

"You mean — everything I see is yours?"

"Yes, my little son. This may be hard for you to understand, little ram, but I am also called the Infinite, the one who created all of this that you see and more!"

"Gosh, I never knew there was a voice out there. I run up here every day to see the world in the sky. Is it your world, too?"

"Yes, my son, it is — my world that I created just for you."

"It is?"

"It is!"

"Did you make it for my brothers and sisters too?"

"Yes."

"And my mother — I know you made it for my mother because she told me about the sky and that it would always be there every morning when I wake up. She's real smart, you know. She knows a lot of stuff that I don't."

"Yes, young ram. Charles, you should listen to your mother more often. She has the wisdom that only a mother can. She carries the wisdom of the world deep inside her heart."

"She does?" Charles replied incredulously.

"She does, my son. She carries it in a special place inside her heart, a place I created for all your family to go in to be with me."

"Really? It's in her heart? Do I have a place like that in my heart?"

"Yes you do, Charles. Every little ram has one, every mother and every father, sister, and brother — you all have that special place inside of you!"

"Where is it? I'm looking, but I don't see anything. Where is it?"

"It is there deep, deep within your heart, too, Charles. If you don't see it, close your eyes for a minute. In your mind, go deep to the core of your being. Don't worry that your eyes don't see anything — reach out with your feelings."

"My feelings? What do you mean? What are 'feelings'?"

"Charles, you love your mother, isn't that right?"

"Well yes, of course I do. And she's a good mother too. She watches out for me!"

"Yes, yes, I know, Charles." The big voice seemed to laugh. "Slow down a minute. When you love your mother, that's called a feeling. You 'feel' love for her, right? So when you are looking for that special place in your heart, feel that love, be with it, and you will automatically be in that special place that I have created. And you will be there with me."

"I will?"

"You always will, my son — I always will, for I am in the sky, I am in the rain, I am in the sunlight. I made the hills and the rivers and that mountain you can see far in the distance. And I made you too, Charles."

Our little ram looked surprised. "You did? You made me?"

"I made you too, little ram. I made you too."

"Wow! I never knew this before. I never knew I could talk to the sky! And I never knew that it could talk back to me — wow!"

"You should go back home, little ram. Your mother is looking for you, and she wants to know that you're safe. You run on home now, and we'll talk again tomorrow, okay?"

"Okay!" Charles shouted, already running down the hill. "Okay, see you tomorrow! Okay!" His little voice faded away as he ran down the little hill.

"Okay!" rumbled the voice from the hill. "See you tomorrow!"

Charles woke up the very next morning in a bit of a daze. He was a tiny bit confused. He had not told his mother about the great voice yet because he wasn't sure she would believe him. He thought and thought, and he pondered (yes, in our fable even rams can ponder!) about what had happened the previous afternoon.

On the one hand, when he was talking to the voice, it had seemed so real. But when he got home, he started to doubt himself. "Was I really talking to … the sky?" he thought. "I'm not sure that's even possible. It's pretty hard for a young ram like me to figure. Mama can't talk to the sky. Why would it talk to me? I'm just a little guy. Maybe it should have talked to my Uncle Cecil. Uncle Cecil is very old and very smart, and he usually knows the answers to questions that Mama doesn't know. But then, Uncle Cecil can hardly walk anymore, and he sleeps all the time, so I guess that's why the sky didn't talk to him. When I go up the hill again, will the voice be there today too? I mean, it said it would be there. It promised! So I'm just going to run up there again today, because, you know, I still have to make sure that the sky is there too. I'm a little afraid to, though. What if it's not there like it said it would be? What will I do? Oh, I hope so much that it will be, though. I think it likes me, and it didn't care that I'm so little and so young. I guess that's all right too. Okay okay, I'm going to run up there right now. I'm not going to be afraid. I'm not a 'fraidy cat — not me! I am brave little Charles, that's who I am! It'll be okay. The voice from the sky will be there. I know it'll be there waiting to talk to me."

And with that, Charles went charging out in his usual "little ram" way, head-butting the gate and running out ahead of the others. His mother just watched him and sighed. "I don't know what's gotten into that boy lately," she lamented. "He's even more exuberant than before! Such an impetuous young ram! Ah, me." She sighed and went out to the pasture to eat.

Charles ran up the hill to see if the voice was still there along with the sky. He arrived at the top of the hill and looked out to see the beautiful vista. And, as usual, he said to himself, "It's here! It's still here! I see it! I see it!"

"Yes, you do, Charles. You always see it — you just don't know you do!"

Charles sighed in relief. The voice was still there, just as it said it would be.

"Hi," Charles ventured shyly. "I wasn't sure you'd still be here when I got back up here today. I mean, I was hoping you would be. I was really hoping."

"Do not ever worry about that, little ram, for you are small in size but big in heart. You have courage and patience, and an eagerness to know more about your world. You braved the snowstorm to come up to see our world. You would not be stopped or deterred in any way, for your courage is admirable. You are 'Charles with the Stalwart Heart.' Do you want to know why I chose you, my son? I heard you asking that question."

"You did?"

"I did indeed! That day when you braved the storm, I wanted to speak to you that day, but I thought that it would be too much for you. That was a little foolhardy — you know that, don't you?" the voice boomed out.

"Well, yes, I guess it was. Mama said it was. But I just couldn't help myself! And I was afraid that if I didn't see the sky, it wouldn't be there the next day! And I couldn't bear for that to happen. I just couldn't!"

The voice laughed. "Little one, you never need to be afraid that the sky — or I — wouldn't be there, for I am always there for you, Charles. And I'm there for your entire family. In fact, I'm there for the entire world. Always and forever. There is never a time when I am not. Do not ever be afraid of that again. Your mother was right, young Charles. The sky and I are always there, waiting for you to discover us. I never move, and I will always be here. Whenever you seek me, you will find me. Wherever you look, there will I be. And however you find me, I will be there. I will always be there." The powerful voice rumbled from the sky again. "I am in the sky. I am in the ocean. I am in everything, and I am above everything at the same time. You see, Charles, being in my creation does not sully me. My life, my spirit, is in all things, big and small. I am in the tallest mountain, and I am in the tiniest and most delicate of flowers. I am in the waters of the great ocean, and at the bottom of it in its greatest depths. I am there. Where there is no light, I bring light. And where there is no life, I bring it. And where there is no love, I am there too, for it can be no other way. I am eternal, Charles — I am eternal."

Charles was dumbfounded. He did not know what to say. Finally he found his voice, sounding timid and small. "Please … what does 'eternal' mean?"

"It means that I never die, Charles. It means that there is no death. It means that I love you all, forever and always. It cannot be otherwise."

"Oh," was all Charles could think to say. "You love me? Does that mean you'll be here tomorrow when I come back? Uh … I have to go now. Mama is calling for me."

"Yes, she is, Charles. Run back home, and you can talk to me again tomorrow, and every day. I'm here. I'm always here for you, son. Now run along."

"Okay. See you — and the sky — tomorrow!" With that, Charles scampered away.

He ran home, as his mother had indeed called him. He had been gone longer than usual, and she was worried. "Charles, what on earth are you doing up there on that hill for all that time? I saw you up there just gazing at the sky for what seemed like forever. Are you okay? What were you doing up there?" she asked.

"Oh, Maaa-maaa," he bleated in an anxious voice. "I'm okay. Am I in trouble?"

"No, my dear, you're not. I'm not mad at you. But you've been running up the hill lately and staying there. Before, when you ran up the little hill, I always knew that you would be down soon, after you checked on the sky. But lately you've been spending more time up there. It seemed like an hour today! And now I'm going to ask you, Charles, is anything wrong? Are you talking to someone up there, because for a minute there, I could have sworn that you were almost talking to someone."

Charles started to cry, but he quickly stopped the tears. After all, he was a "big boy" now — the voice had said so — but he was terrified that if he told his mother what he was really doing up there, she would make him stop going for good. In his heart he longed to tell her — to tell her all about the voice and what it said to him — what he could remember, at least! So he hedged a little bit. "Maaa-maaa, would you be mad at me if I told you I was talking to someone up there? Would you? Would you get real mad and not let me go back, because if you do, then I can't tell you. But I want to, Maaa-maaa. I want to so much!" he said, tearfully.

"Why, honey! Why are you crying?"

"I'm not crying!" Charles shouted in denial. "I'm a big boy now, and big boys don't cry!"

"Honey, of course I won't get mad at you. I was just wondering what you were doing up there these last few days, that's all. I'm worried about you."

"Oh, Maaa-maaa!" Charles burst into tears again. "I so want to tell you! I do so want to tell you everything! Please promise you won't make me stop going if I tell you. Promise!"

"Okay, honey, okay. Whatever it is, we will just talk it out together, you and me, okay?"

"Okay, Maaa-maaa." He stopped crying and looked up hopefully. She put his head on her shoulder and comforted him. He sniffed loudly a couple of times, wiped his eyes again, and summoning all his courage, said, "Promise you won't make me stop going if I tell you. Promise!"

"Okay."

"Maaa-maaa, I have something to tell you. And you're probably going to think it's weird, but I have — I have been talking to someone up there, Maaa-maaa. It ... I was just standing there, looking at the sky and the world, 'cause it's so beautiful, Maaa-maaa."

He took a deep breath and continued on. "A voice started to talk to me, Maaa-maaa — a voice in the sky. It talked to me and knew my name and everything. And, Maaa-maaa ... it just seemed so natural to talk to it. I wasn't scared at all. I really wasn't, Maaa-maaa. It told me lots of things — it even mentioned you, Maaa-maaa!"

The words came tumbling out in a rush, almost stumbling over themselves. He was so excited now. He was going to tell her everything — but wait! She hadn't said anything yet. "Maaa-maaa ... Maaa-maaa, are you okay?" he asked. A sharp stab of fear assailed him again. "Maaa-maaa, say something! Are you mad?"

She looked up at him and very gently took him in her arms and stroked his fleece. "Oh, Charles," was all she could say.

Charles raised his head and looked at her closely. Was she okay? She didn't seem mad at all, but she was acting strangely. She raised her head, looked him straight in the eye, and said, "Charles. Charles, honey, I have something to tell you too," she said very quietly. "When I was a young ewe, just about your same age, the sky started talking to me too. But I never did answer it back — I was too scared! And you say that it spoke to you and you answered back? And you had a conversation with it? Did you really? Please, tell me everything. Tell me everything you talked about. I want to know. I need to know!"

"Oh, Maaa-maaa, really? Did you really hear the voice, too?" He was so excited! "And you're not mad at me? Yippee!" He started jumping up and down and kicking his legs in the air! His mother, who had been so serious a moment before, started laughing and laughing. She was happy, too!

A great burden had been lifted from both of them because, you see, Charles's mother had heard the voice, too, but she rejected it. It had stopped talking to her after that, and she later regretted that she had been too afraid to communicate with it. She had even told herself that it was nothing, and over the many years since, she had begun to wonder if she had just imagined it. But here was Charles — her precious Charles — telling her that he had heard the voice too. And not only had he heard it, but he had talked to it! She needed to know desperately what it said to him, her little Charles. And it was at this point that she realized that it had been a gift — a precious gift — and her son had it too!

Charles gazed in wonderment at his mother. Why had she never told him? Why had she never told his other brothers and sisters either? It was a mystery he had to solve!

"Maaa-maaa, did you really mean it when you said that you heard the voice too?" he asked her.

"Yes, dear. I did."

"Well, why didn't you just talk to it? It's not that scary. Okay, it is — just a little — but why? What really happened, Maaa-maaa?"

"Oh, honey, yes, I did hear the voice. And yes, I was very scared! I was afraid my mother would find out and that I would be in big trouble too. It was just a lot of things, honey, and I was so young …"

"But I am too, Maaa-maaa. I'm young too, but I'm not scared. I told you: I'm not a 'fraidy cat — no! When it started talking to me, it felt really soothing, Maaa-maaa — like when you hold me and make me feel better when I'm sad or tired. You're a good mother, Maaa-maaa, and I think the voice is good too. It must be, 'cause it's talking from the sky, and you'd have to be good to be up there, or else you might fall down. Maybe it floats or something …" His voice trailed off in thought.

"Oh, honey." Charles's mother smiled. She went inside herself for a moment. "Maybe it does — float, I mean. What do you think, sweetie?" She rubbed his head again, scratching between his ears. "My, you're getting so big! You're already getting horns! Soon you won't be 'little Charles' anymore. You'll be 'Charles the Mighty Ram' — big enough to leap small hills in a single bound!" They both laughed. "Come," she said. "Let's go inside for now. It's getting late, and we're both really tired. Let's keep talking in the morning, okay honey?"

"Okay, Maaa-maaa. I love you."

"I love you too, honey. I love you too!"

And with that, they both went under the enclosure and slept very hard. Charles's mother used to hear the sky talk too, but she had never told anyone. She had kept it secret for many years not only out of anticipation of disapproval but also out of prudence and good sense. Since she had only heard it one time, she had told herself that it wasn't important. She even, as the memory faded, began to wonder if she had imagined hearing the voice in the sky. In fact, she did not tell her children about it at all — not because she was afraid of losing their love, but because she truly did not know if she had just been going crazy and hearing voices in her head. She had simply felt that adopting a "wait and see" attitude was much more prudent and the right thing to do. So her motivation for keeping it hidden was primarily familial — for the good of the family.

Charles woke up early the next morning. His mother was not yet awake, so he had time to think. He lay there close to his mother, turning the conversation of the preceding night over and over in his mind. He cuddled closely against her warm body in the early morning air. What a day that had been yesterday! He was still dancing on air in his mind and heart. Two good things had happened: The voice had been there again, and his mother wasn't mad at him. He knew now that he could tell her anything and she would understand. What a wonderful mother he had! He snuggled into her. She was just beginning to awaken.

"Maybe we could go up the hill together today," he lay there thinking. "Would she go with me? Oh, would she really?" He started getting excited again. "Oh, that would be so wonderful — me and Mama together on the hill listening to the voice. Maybe then she could explain what exactly it was saying. There was so much he said yesterday that I can scarcely remember all of it. Let's see … it said that it was in everything. I remember that. And it said something about a special place in our hearts. Then, oh gosh — what was it? Something about feelings. It talked about a lot of stuff I had never heard of before, but Mama will know. I hope I can talk her into going with me. Oh, will she really come? Yippee!"

Charles's thoughts were starting to run rampant again. He didn't realize it, but he had been wriggling around while he was busy thinking, and by now his mother was fully awake. "Charles!" she said sharply, "What are you doing? You can't seem to lie still!" She peered into his face. He popped open his eyes and looked up at her sweetly.

"Maaa-maaa, you're awake! Oh, Maaa-maaa, I was just thinking about yesterday and was getting so excited again!" And then, very impetuously, he blurted out, "Maaa-maaa! Do you want to go to the hill with me today? It could be lots of fun."

His mother stood up, shook herself off, and then said, "We'll see, honey. Now let's go eat our morning meal first. Then we can talk some more."

Charles was very eager to get out to the hill to see the sky and hear the voice, but this morning he heeded his mother and walked calmly out with her and the rest of the flock to the meadows, where they leisurely started chewing on the grass. He put his head down with her and waited as patiently as a young ram could as she chewed. Finally she stopped, looked up at him, and said, with a wink in her eye, "Don't you think it's about time for us to go up the hill, Charles?"

"Oh yes, Maaa-maaa, oh yes! Let's go!" And he took off like a shot. It was an amusing sight to see Charles running and prancing up the hill, his mother slowly plodding along after him. In his exuberance, he would run up the hill, then down to his mother, then up the hill again, and back down to her. She had never seen him this excited before.

"Do you really think you'll hear the voice, Maaa-maaa? Do you? Do you?" Charles asked.

His mother just kept going slowly but steadily up the hill. She was getting a little older and it took her longer, but she persisted, and soon she was standing on the top of the hill with Charles.

"Look, Maaa-maaa, look! Look at the world. You can see the whole world from here — did you know that?"

"No, honey, I didn't. But I see what you mean. It is very beautiful up here, and you can see very far away. I haven't been up on a steep hill in a long time, honey." She was so tired that she folded her legs up under her and sat down for a minute. Then there it was — a sound — a rumbling sound a little like thunder, but friendly.

"Hello, Charles! I see you have brought your mother. You don't know this, but she and I talked many years ago when I spoke to her out in the fields late one afternoon. Do you remember, my dear?" the voice said.

Charles's mother looked up quickly, glanced at her son, and replied, timidly at first, "Yes, I remember you. I had almost forgotten about it since it was so long ago …" Her voice trailed off.

"And what do you remember, dear lady? Think deeply and find my words deep in your memory. Do you know now?" the voice said.

Charles broke in and shouted, "Do you hear him, Maaa-maaa? Do you hear him?"

She nodded solemnly at her son and then addressed the voice, trembling, "I don't think I remember what it was you said to me — only that I had heard a voice in the sky and wondered if something was wrong with me. That I do remember. That, I remember."

"You were so very young. Let me help to see if I can jog your memory."

As she was sitting there, a thought popped into her head. "Oh, my goodness. I do remember now. It was an invitation — an invitation to come back to that same meadow and talk with you. I heard you say very distinctly, 'I am the voice of the heavens, the Infinite, the All. Come and listen to my voice and hear the wisdom of the ages. Come and sit at my feet and hear my voice again, for I am your eternal father, the Almighty, and I come to bring you joy, love, and brotherhood for all! Come!'"

She looked up at the sky and burst into tears. "Why could I not remember these wonderful words? Why did I run from you? Oh, I wish I had gone back now. I wish I had gone back!"

"Hear me again," the voice said, "and listen, for I have come again to you. Your little son, Charles, has helped to bring me back to you, little mother. You were the one I wanted to talk to, and you got scared and ran away. At the precise moment we could have had a relationship, you turned away. I was very regretful that you never returned, so I waited for Charles here to find me in the sky. Now I am not really in the sky, but I created it, so when people come searching for me, I am here. It is a place they expect me to be, so I am here for you — and for him — and for everyone who sincerely seeks me."

Now she felt bold. "Can we come up here every day to talk to you? Will you be here every day like Charles told me?"

"Yes, my dear. Yes. Come to see me every day, and we will have that talk we never had before, for I am your eternal best friend, your father, your mother, your sister, and your brother, for I am family. That is what I longed to tell you all those many years ago. But that is the past and will stay in the past. At this present moment, you are here with me, and that is all that matters now. You and Charles may come and visit and talk with me any time. You are welcome here always!"

With that, she looked at Charles and said, "I guess we're coming every day from now on."

Charles jumped up and down for joy. "Maaa-maaa, you heard it. You heard it too. Didn't I tell you how special it is coming up the hill and talking to it?"

"Yes, you did, honey! Yes, you did."

And with that, they traveled back down the hill to finish eating.

, , ,

The Relationship of Man and Man

So it is in your world's history of man-to-man relationships ("man" meaning men and women — all of humanity) that we find there are certain potentials that all people incarnating on the planet carry with them as they come in: an equal propensity for good or ill, light or dark, peace or struggle — both within each person and within individual and group relationships. There is also mass consciousness with which each person has to contend.

Now, as people grow up and go out into the world, they learn many things, but what we find with humankind is that there is a certain plethora of relationships versus the dynamic of each person's personality in regard to the personal profile, arc, and identity coupled with the potentialities for each. In simpler terms, you are born into a world of choices and options.

The Moment, the Now, and Mastery

Each choice that is made in each present moment identifies who you are, or who you think you are, in that moment. And in those moment-to-moment choices, your life unfolds, either opening or closing to certain situations, people, or options in your life. Each moment of decision or indecision, right or wrong, left or right, informs your next step, and at some point, you will start to realize that the only true power to alter or sustain a path or a relationship lies within that moment of potentiality — the now! It is the fulcrum point of true wisdom and the beginning of mastery.

7

The Courier

This is a story about a courier. She is a person with whom the quality of service is very high. She starts each day early and goes about her morning routine with love and happiness for all in her heart. Her children have all grown up, and she is on her own. She sent them out into life with the knowledge that she had done the best that she could at the time, with the secure feeling that they were all right and would do well.

Now, this courier was not always a person with love in her heart. When she was very young, she was known to be brooding and depressive, driven by anxiety and self-pity. She had been very focused on herself, as people who are in pain often are. However, as she matured, she started growing and healing as a person, both inside and out. And when she had her first child, she was blessed with a tremendous inner healing that strengthened her and made it possible for her to start to really learn about unselfishness. For what she would not or could not do for herself, she found she could do out of tremendous love for her child, and she grew by leaps and bounds.

Love and Service

As this courier continued to learn about love and service, she was gradually able to leave her old tortured self behind and become a new person — the person inside of her that she always knew she could be. She started to shine her inner love and light out to the whole world. Considering the world to be just an extension of her family, she gradually saw that the whole world *was* her family and that she was never alone. Her partner in this life, a man of high integrity and honor, helped blaze a path in front of her, for he was a man who had lived his whole life in service and dedication to others — to his family, to his work. In all his day-to-day dealings, he was a master when it came to service. Our courier learned from him many, many things about the true meaning of service and the many applications of it on a daily basis.

So she would awaken every morning with love, service, humility, and the joy of living in her heart, and, by and by, she found a job in which she could use these skills every day. She discovered that she was a courier, a messenger to bring peace and love to all beings — a bridge of sorts. She lived out each day eager to love and serve, sharing her life with her partner of many lifetimes as they walked each day in love, respect, and honor of each other and of their supreme service to the world.

Her Personal Journey: Finding Her Life's Mission

The courier's life mission was to find love and light for herself in this life, as she had been unable to in many lives before. Delicate and contrite from many selfish lifetimes, she searched for meaning and relationships. And in this search, she slowly began to find her way through the maze of her life. Through great difficulties, rejection, and ridicule, she gradually found her way emotionally and spiritually. Gifted with the voice of song, she found being in choirs and in churches to be a great source of beauty, inspiration, comfort, strength, and friendship with like minds and hearts. This became her sanctuary, for no matter how hard her life became, the choir setting lifted her soul and it began to unfold its wings. A sensitive soul, she longed for friendship and normalcy, for it happened that she was struck by a speech impediment. But she was determined to speak normally again someday.

From Depression to Love for All

However, severe depression had also set in, and she felt lost and very alone, and would cry herself to sleep often in those early years. Then out of the darkness she read a book that opened a great light in her mind and heart, and her soul soared to new heights at the inspiring words and uplifting message. It made sense to her and gave her new meaning in her life. She found the strength to carry on, finally realizing that her difficult struggles had meaning and purpose.

On and on she struggled, with many, many setbacks. She continued to encounter a lot of losses in her life, but with a developing identity in God, she made her way through a difficult relationship with pain that was karmic in origin. She learned many things about herself and people before she finally found a way through to love instead of hate, forgiveness instead of anger, and harmony within herself instead of chaos.

Her children, although many, were a tremendous source of love, giving of self, and even friendship for her. She had begun on a healing path with the birth of the first child. Her heart filled with deep love for the child, and for each one as they came, for as she raised them and played with them, her own child within began to blossom, grow, and heal itself, for she finally found that unselfish giving of love brings that love right back.

A Carrier

Now, the woman in our story is not a courier in the traditional sense, as in a mail courier or someone who works for the legal or court system. She is not a letter bearer, a document bearer, or even a person who delivers packages, boxes, or certified mail of any type. She is different in that she brings messages and transmissions from a different arena — she is a carrier of sorts, like a royal carrier from a kingdom far away in a remote area of the world. As such, she appears, ready and willing to deliver words of wisdom and many gifts from that remote kingdom to the world at large. But the deliveries arrive a bit like babies do — at their own time and choosing, and often not on any kind of schedule but their own. And she is ever ready to birth them, adding her love and joy to them as she blesses them and sends them on their way. Like flowers budding and opening, like a sudden rainfall, they come to wash away the old, bringing new awakenings and new insights to a weary world ever renewing itself on eager shores. Urgent messages from a faraway place — brothers reaching out to brothers, sisters reaching out to sisters — uniting families long separated. Now the appointed time has come.

And so the courier waits. She waits until she is called, then rises up to the task at hand, faithful and diligent, and she pours her own pure heart into it. The job she performs is one of great honor, and she is not sure she is worthy to do it, but the king picked her for a specific reason and has full confidence in her abilities, which are more than she herself realizes. Don't get us wrong here — she is not a perfect person yet, but the king knows that she is the right person for the job.

Now, this courier is the type of person who obeys instructions well. She is diligent in getting every word of a transmission to be sent accurately as if through a fine-toothed comb, making sure that the words, and the *intent* of those words and ideas, are set forth with absolute accuracy and precision. She prepares herself every morning with prayer and meditation according to the dictates of each day, like how a nest is lovingly prepared for new little hatchlings.

She would at times receive instructions and tutorials about how to be a better courier, better ways of packaging and so on, as she went. Then she would pray over each package to be delivered and lovingly send each on its way, sometimes joining the other packages, sometimes not. Whatever the divine prerogative for the day, she gladly and dutifully performs. It is a learning process for her as well — the kind of job that as you grow personally, emotionally, and spiritually, you are able to bring more of yourself to any task at hand.

A Messenger

Far from perfect at first, the courier grew to have greater respect and honor for each of the packages and messages she carried. She became a "divine messenger" of sorts — not in actuality, but clearly in essence, word, and deed. This was incredibly important to each project, each delivery, and each package. She had the potentiality of a great courier and worked at becoming better and more dedicated. That potentiality quotient increased until she saw in herself the probability that sprang into full reality.

The courier has the unique requirements for the responsibilities of her job, but she also has something that is equally important to the task: discernment and good judgment in nearly all circumstances. There are times when she becomes very human but is able to discern and correct problems, situations, and even egocentric behavior on her part as part of the ongoing learning processes of her life. She is not one to rest on her laurels, but she remains ever vigilant to her own very human weaknesses and vicissitudes. She is humble and forthright enough to admit and correct mistakes as she goes about her life, for she also knows that whatever affects her life personally affects her work, for — again — all is one, is it not? She does not allow things like moods, unforeseen circumstances, tiredness, aches, pains, and so on to get in the way of her dedication to her job. She practiced these skills when she became a parent and knows deep within herself that she became a better, more loving, giving, and selfless person, because as a mother, these things were required inherently of her. She rose to the task, both as a mother and in her current job as a chief courier.

Living Life in Reverse, a Common Human Trait

We also want to talk about our courier's penchant for doing things in reverse sometimes, which is another very human trait — saying no to something she could have said yes to, and saying yes to certain things when she should have had the courage to say no. Making the "correct" decisions had always been a difficult task for her, but when she started learning to say no to the relative trivia in her life, it enabled and emboldened her to say yes to the things that were better for her, such as the job of courier. And being a good courier sometimes means that she has to make personal sacrifices, but in the end she is better able to do her job — a job that was actually created for her.

She is the type of person who always allows others to speak their minds and hearts, and she always turns a conversation around in a way that will most benefit that person. Far from finding fault, she encourages them to look within themselves while remaining unattached to the outcome of a conversation. She loves to help people, and in her job as a courier, she has many times gone above and beyond to accomplish or finish a task, even to the point of going back as many times as it takes to make certain that it is correct *and* correctly understood. A person with a big heart, she declares each morning that she loves everyone — and she truly means it. This is a long way from the way she was at the beginning of this life. Remember, we told you how depressed she could be at times, feeling utterly alone. Over a period of time, she worked with herself, constantly seeking to improve. Little by little, she reached the point of not only loving everyone — and indeed, all of creation — but she finally found a way to love herself too.

Now, by this time the world had changed around her, not only in the immediate vicinity of her orbit, but the world itself had changed, wrapping itself around and through her life. What happened was millions more like her had also encountered early difficulties and hardships and had found their way back from heartache to love, from isolation to fellowship and understanding, from soul-hunger to satiety, from feeling lost to being found, and from death to life. In doing so, the courier and the millions like her had effected profound changes on this planet.

Letting Self-Doubt Go

We have shown you, the reader, many different sides and facets of the person we are calling the courier, but now we shall share with you a different side of her. As a lightworker, she first heard her call when she was much younger than she is now. In the beginning of this spiritual journey, we want our readers to realize that she did not recognize the gift within herself at first. Her low self-esteem and misunderstanding of piety led her to doubt herself. She doubted that anything she could do would ever be anything of significance to the world. She was still mired in negativity and the inherent, unavoidable self-focus that it brought. She was very dutiful in service to her children and husband, but she did not see the larger picture or her possible place in it at the time.

We would have, and could have, had a much longer association with her, a productive relationship over many, many years, but just as she was beginning to blossom and come out, she pulled back into her old self-doubts and laziness and let it go. The life that she is stepping into now could have begun so much sooner, and many, many opportunities, associations, and rewarding experiences would not have been lost to her. She is very aware of this fact. The reason we bring it up, however, dear reader, is to show you parts of her life and how decisions she made — and didn't make — affected the path of her life. This is not so much to criticize as to use her life as an example of how much better it is to truly see and take hold of life's opportunities when they first arrive instead of going into so much doubt that you take yourself out of a game in which you could have had a major part in making things better for all.

Write Yourself Back into Life

As we have said, she is keenly aware of this story and hopes that in its telling someone reading this will not make the same mistakes she made years ago — that they will not miss out on as much as she did. Our lesson to you all today is this: This is a fable of sorts, but the courier's story is so common that we share it to encourage those who, like her, have so much to give but are afraid to give it! See yourself as important in the scheme of things, and write yourself *into*, not out of, the history of this Earth.

We want to point out to our readers that this courier was not the kind of person you would traditionally think of as a lightworker. She was definitely a person who, in the Hindu sense, would be called a "householder." When she was small, there was little about her that you would have thought was special, smart, or extraordinary. In fact, in many ways she was a very ordinary child — self-focused, immature, and petty in the way children can be. She was also a very lonely child with an odd personality, and her peers generally avoided her. The opposite of popular, she was usually the "nobody" in her crowd — and in her life too. And she knew it. But somewhere along the way on the path of her life, she engaged and started to understand her life more, especially in a spiritual sense.

Contemplative and philosophical, she found her way through many books. Books became her friends when she didn't have any. Books helped her to understand the vicissitudes and the up-and-down currents of her life. Books lifted her up and inspired her to be something greater than she was, to move beyond the normal scope of what the world offered. She reached for the stars. With God's help, she pushed herself to recover from depression and stop stuttering, and she spent many years in self-improvement and study. She did this by learning to heal and open her heart. She also strove to keep herself inspired.

The Dark Night of the Soul: Finding Your Way Out

This is not to say that her life went straight upward from very ordinary to extraordinary; there were many hills, valleys and long, dry periods when she would "backslide" and rejoin the confusion and chaos felt by the masses. These were her times of darkness — her desert times, her "dark night of the soul" times. But somehow, within herself, she always found her way back, like hearing an inner beacon that was ignored for a while and then you suddenly realize is there.

So, with many stops and starts, and an extremely inauspicious beginning, by constantly pulling herself up by her bootstraps, she made herself into something more — the caring, emotionally healthy, special person she is today. She is a living example of what can be accomplished in a lifetime if you want it enough. Even after repeated stumbles, she kept getting back up and continued to improve, learn lessons, and move forward. She was not content to be ordinary. She wanted more out of herself and out of her life, and she found it.

Lifetimes Elsewhere

We have referred to our courier as someone with many personal challenges, and one of them was just being here on Earth at this time. She had many lifetimes in which she found it difficult to be on Earth in the third dimension. Part of the reason she found it so difficult was because she was originally a being of the higher realms; she was originally from the star system of Sirius, where life is much gentler and more love-based. Everyone there is taught and guided from birth about how sacred and important the balance and harmoniousness of all life is.

The people from Sirius have already progressed through the stages that Earth is going through now — although much more mildly — so they are more advanced in every way. They are taught from birth how to live in harmony and balance with nature; they are taught how to live in love, harmony, and peace with each other and in loving harmony with the needs of the life they all share on their planet. They are not perfect by any means, but by Earth standards, they are much, much further down the road.

We know you have all heard this analogy before, but it is a good one: If the advancement of a planet was a football field, the Sirian culture as a whole would be on the opponent's 30 yard line, meaning 70 yards gained with 30 yards to go. The people of Earth are on the 30 yard line, meaning 30 yards gained and 70 yards to go. We think this will help you, dear reader, to realize how much farther they, and you, still have to go, especially in respect to other civilizations and planetary systems — which, by the way, are very, very many, too numerous to be counted.

So our courier, having been used to a more advanced culture, always had a hard time being an "Earth person" for the simple fact that in past lifetimes — but certainly this one also — she felt Earth and its people were barbaric, cold, lonely, and extremely disconnected. And by barbaric, we don't just mean physically barbaric — we mean emotionally and ideologically barbaric in the things that are accepted on Earth as normal, such as war, racism, the dual scourges of poverty and starvation, and the rape and disrespect of the planet and all life here.

Planetary Unity: The Law of One

Each time she was here she would, at a very deep level, long for that other world where people were just nicer and there was never anger, war, or strife. A place where there was planetary unity — not in the utilitarianism sense of the word, but a gentle, loving, nonjudgmental unity. Now, this did not so much mean one centralized government, because all people are taught to be self-governing, but it is more in a sense of what we mentioned before: one main moral precept for all, one that is implicitly agreed on and implemented by all in their daily lives. It was a code of conduct, so to speak, but with a quality to it that encompassed a much broader range and scope. This was called the "law of one," and it had worked well on other planets for many millennia.

So our courier was used to and sensed deep within that there was something more, something better. She sensed and knew deeply that the status quo of the way things are done here didn't have to be the way it was. It was, and is, inwardly barbaric and unacceptable to her how many things are taken for granted or accepted as "unalterable givens"; she knew with every fiber of her being that these things did not necessarily need to be so. So she was very unhappy at times, but she wasn't sure why. Now, however, after her many years of study and reflection, she knows exactly why.

Destiny, Potential, and Free Will

In telling any story of this kind and dealing, basically, with a real person, as we are in this fable, there is always an element of surprise and possible disappointment. The disappointment lies in the fact that a real person may *choose* to not fulfill their potential, not see the glory in front of them, not rise to the occasion, or not see themselves contributing in any way. So their destiny, from a freewill perspective, may not have happened.

The person we have described as the courier almost lost her job before she started it, as she did not recognize and realize her great strengths years earlier, so she almost abdicated the position of courier that had been tailor-made for her long, long before she incarnated.

So great was her lack of self-worth that even when she had the opportunity to continue her training, she let it go by the wayside so much so that her employer had despaired of ever being able to use her. The great surprise was that, at the eleventh hour of her life, she re-engaged in her training just in time to get back on schedule and to be used as the main courier/carrier. This was an act of free will on her part, and there was literally rejoicing in heaven when she made it. A life-ending illness that she had self-created in her "desert time" was quickly abated, and her scheduled exit passed over as she received and engaged the job for which she had, unknown to her, been prepared for.

The Use of Will

The use of the will in our modern age is something that is not quite fully understood, especially in Western culture. Willpower is primarily only understood in terms of its connection to the breaking of bad habits or in connection with food, drink, smoking, or other things in your daily lives that entice and sometimes enslave you. For example, if you have strong willpower, you can break these vices' hold over you.

What we want to touch on here is the use of your will in a much larger context. Human will these days is largely like an unused muscle, barely thought of in your day-to-day dealings. But in a larger sense, you are on a planet of free will where the proper use of will is seldom taught or practiced. This is unfortunate, since in a freewill environment, proper or right use of will should be taught to children from day one. For example, what would be termed a right use of will could be presented first as how to make better choices in, say, food selection, which hopefully would be modeled by parents and caregivers. Children can be taught simple things at first, like choosing to eat an apple rather than a piece of candy, or a vegetable they like instead of chips. As they grow up, then, and become more cognizant, they will start to see that certain choices, or the way they use their will, are better than others, and this strengthens their willpower. You get the idea.

Freewill Environment and Choice

Living as you do in a freewill environment has much more influence and impact on each of you than you realize. A large part of the "power" in willpower, then, comes from the moment. Within each moment is where the power is, as has been taught in many other books. But it is *in* that present moment that your will comes into play. Let's, for instance, say that a smoker uses his free will to make a momentous decision — that of not smoking — in a single moment. He then is using his free will at that powerful moment to "pivot on a dime" and made a 180-degree turn from the previous present moment to affect a life-changing, and possibly life-saving, moment, isn't he? He used his will to do it — a choice! He literally "willed" himself back to health and back into the game, back to that longer life he really wanted to have. He saved himself by the proper use of his will. And the *power* of it was the power of the moment. Can you see from this example how important the use of your will can be? It can be everything!

Divine Will

If you use that human will in conjunction with divine will, the flexing of that muscle can be very strong indeed. The great yogis of India learned the proper and right use of will in their first yoga lesson. They were taught to combine, or become one with, the divine will in order to accomplish what are seen as great feats on Earth. Their yogic training began with the simple lesson of the proper use of will.

Going back to our allegory of the will as a muscle, then, we think it will be easier to understand the broader use of the will and how it can be incorporated into daily use. You see, you don't realize it, but everyone technically uses will every day without realizing it. When you get up in the morning and *choose* to have a cup of coffee, for example, you just used your will. You made a choice — that is the use of will. You choose to drive to work a certain way, or to go to a certain gas station you like because the prices are lower, or to go to the store and buy liquor and bring it home. That is the use of will, is it not? So you exercised that muscle a little bit, didn't you?

Now, when you were buying the more economical gasoline, would you say that that was a good choice? Yes, we believe most people would agree that that's a "right" decision, or at least a better one than, say, having to fill up a gas-guzzling vehicle that requires a more expensive type of fuel. On the other hand, would you say that buying that liquor was a good use of your will? Maybe so, maybe not — we think there would be a split decision on that one. If the liquor is bought with the intent of social drinking, there may be no harm here. But it changes, doesn't it? If the liquor is bought by a person or for a person who is, or is becoming, addicted, then you would say that was *not* a good use of will. That momentary decision to purchase the liquor would be an improper use of free will, would you not agree?

The Paralyzed Will: Addiction

Now we want to talk briefly about what addiction really means: the enslavement of a person's free will. The will is no longer free, is it? It has been deadened and slammed into submission, to put it one way. To put it another way, it has been paralyzed and neutralized so that the person thus enslaved is no longer using that muscle at all. That muscle is flaccid and just lying there atrophying, is it not? So we see here an example of someone who has given up using free will. In this case, it is no longer free and is owned by the addictive substance and the addictive process itself. In this case, the addiction owns you, and it owns your will. It drives you, and you have given all of your power, your will, over to it. It is an extremely sad and tragic situation, and it takes a tremendous amount of energy and the full resuscitation of a person's use of will to backpedal against the power of an addiction/enslavement. Hopefully, a person fully taken over in this manner can regain the healthy use of his or her will and be free again — the natural state for all of us. It's extraordinarily difficult to do, but, of course, well worth the effort.

On the other side of that, we have found that a muscle that is flexed and used regularly — on a daily basis — will continue to grow stronger. Is that not true? So if the will is used in a "right" manner — a better choice than, say, another "not as right" choice — it would be far easier in the long run to just keep those good choices going, would it not? A choice is an in-the-moment act of will. So we *do* use our freewill in-the-moment decisions on a daily basis after all, do we not?

Present Moments: Aware and Awake

Let's talk about something we have not talked much about before. In those moments, those present moments, making that decision requires one other thing of us, doesn't it? It requires a certain level of awareness and awakeness at that moment. And being awake and aware means that in that moment, the proportion of the rightness of the decision depends on how high your level of awareness is — or how awake you truly are. This is where the power truly is, right in that moment — that golden moment of opportunity, of choice, of will.

Right Thinking, "Mindedness," and the Use of Will

We've talked about the negative use of will, such as wrong decisions and the nonuse of will, or willpower in its paralyzed form. So let's move forward and reiterate and summarize our portion on understanding the will and how to use it properly. It helps us, doesn't it, when we make a "right" decision? It can make life a whole lot easier for us and for those around us who are affected, directly or indirectly, by the use or nonuse of our God-given will. Those most affected by our decisions are often the ones who get hurt, are they not?

If you, dear reader, have been reading this and wondering why this section has been included in our book, we will tell you why: because any book that aims to bring "family" together would need to point out and discuss the things that can pull families apart. Now there are many things that can inflict pain on and pull apart families, but the proper knowledge of the use of human free will and a clear concise understanding of it is more than just *essential* in any book that hopes to bring love, unity, and families back together. It is not only essential — it is absolutely *critical* at this point in human evolution on this planet! The proper use of individual and personal willpower by each person living here should be taught from day one and reinforced enough that, by the time children are grown, they can avoid the dangers and pitfalls that befall most generations here. We cannot stress this enough!

And so, dear reader, if you were wondering why we took off on a bit of a tangent, this is the reason why. We love all of you much more than you realize, and it's heartbreaking for us to see the sadness and the misery that a lot of you go through due to the massive misuse and misunderstanding of free will here. We beg all of you to read and reread this section. Put it by your bedside until you can relearn and reteach yourselves what strong, positive, and much easier lives you can really have. And we want you all to have those lives — happy, positive, productive, healthy, and loving lives — not the misery we see so often here. Do yourselves a favor, please, and learn the proper use of will — how and when to flex that muscle — and the whole planet will heave a big sigh of relief.

The Use of Will in Daily Life

Remembering now the principles that you all, dear readers, have been learning in this portion of the chapter about the courier's life, we want to urge all of you to pick up the ball here and take another look at how you use your will in your daily lives — the constant application and awareness of how much you use it or not, without realizing it. You should always be careful not to let others decide things for you, as that would be an abdication of your personal will, would it not be? So try to be more aware, to be more in that momentous and important moment — *the* moment — and we think you will see your life start to move in a more positive direction.

Think before you take that bite of chocolate. *Think* before you make that unnecessary purchase. *Think* before you take that first drink. *Think* before you take that first puff of a cigarette. *Think* before you say yes to something that you know you should say no to! The awareness must take place in these moments. Use that divine gift, your free will, to free yourself, to free up your life for better purposes, better health, better relationships, and a better quality of life than you have ever had before. Teach your children as well. They will thank you later when they realize that they said no to things that could have been very detrimental down the road. Use your freewill muscle and watch it grow and grow. Watch yourself gain confidence. It truly can be transforming, if you let it.

To conclude our story about the courier, she used her free will and at first made what, for her, was an improper use of her will to "drop out." Then, when she re-engaged and went back into training and the life she was meant for, *that* was a better use of her will. And in the end, she started availing herself of the use of the divine will coupled with her own will to help her be all that she could be, both as a person and as a courier. She was able to fulfill her mission, complete her duties as previously planned, and deliver many wonderful things to those she loved so dearly — everybody!

8

The Butler

Once there was a butler — the old-fashioned type of butler that wealthy people used to have to run their mansions and estates. He was quite a dapper chap, and he ran a "tight ship," as the saying goes, and did quite a good job overseeing the staff of a very large estate. As he had been there quite a while, he was well known and respected throughout the world of the gentry that he served.

This butler was called away on an errand, and when he returned, he found that his fellow servants were doing something that was not quite kosher, in his eyes, but it was a relatively small matter. Although it was not quite up to his standards and a slight deviation from protocol, he let it go for the moment with a few misgivings.

As time passed, it seemed this lesser way of doing the job was being emulated by others on the servant staff, as it was a shortcut and took less time. This continued for a while and came to the butler's attention again. He thought to himself, "I must have a meeting of the staff and remind them of the protocol and the reasons for it." One of the reasons the butler enjoyed such a stellar reputation was because of his attention to detail and the thoroughness of the way his plan worked. At the meeting, members of his staff pointed out to him that the task in question — cleaning out the arena where the horses were exercised — did not have to be done every day as his protocol demanded; they said that every other day or so would be fine.

So the butler had a decision to make. Did he bend his rules a bit because his staff did not want to clean the arena every day, or did he adhere to what he knew the lord of the estate wanted, which was that it be cleaned out every day, regardless? He was in quite a quandary over this and told his staff he needed to think about it.

When they all met again the next day, this is what he said to them: "I have given a great deal of thought to the idea of relaxing the rules of protocol regarding the care of the horse arena. I understand it is not a pleasant job, but it is a necessary one for the running of this great estate, and it is the law and desire of the lord that we maintain the grounds of the estate in a pristine manner — cleaned every day. It is considered proper by the lord to maintain this estate in the tried and true way, to the dictates of the owner and lord of it, so I have decided that our staff will continue in the previous manner as before. Our high standards must be upheld at all times. Please be advised." And so the dictate went out. There was grumbling here and there, but the staff continued to uphold the highest standards in their area.

It so happened that a party was planned by the lord of the manor to which many of his fellow gentry were invited. As they arrived early in the evening for the gala, each guest noticed the pristine and beautiful condition of the arena and commented to the lord of the manor that they could not get their staff to keep their horse arenas in such good shape. So they asked him how he was able to get his staff to do it every day. The lord replied that it was due to the high standards the butler had insisted on and that sometimes he would even go out and do it himself or help out on snowy or rainy days to keep it always in good order. Then the lord called in the butler and gave him high praise, saying, "You held to my high standards even when you were tempted to break them, and I know you were sometimes under high pressure and criticism from the other members of the staff. But you did not yield to their pressure, and you stood your ground because you knew that the cleaning of the arena every day was what *I* wanted and required. You shall be highly rewarded!"

* * *

The Lesson: High Standards and Integrity

The story of the butler's loyalty points to more than just that — it also points to a quality of character that we call *integrity*. Of course, he could have caved in to the extreme pressure from his staff, but because of his high moral standards and character, he knew within himself that there was really only one answer to the dilemma: stay the course and see it through, no matter what.

Is it not true that all of you are tempted at times to lower your standards a little bit in order to make it easier for yourselves, to go along with the status quo so that you can be liked or feel more like a part of the group? Or sometimes, are you just a little lazy character-wise, lacking the fundamental backbone you need to stand your ground or stand on principle? When you are speaking about something as important as integrity, isn't it a better idea, or a more "right" choice, to stay pure in thought, word, and deed, especially in the long run? Wouldn't you all feel better about yourselves — later on, especially?

What about your dealings with people in general? Do you expect high standards from yourself? Take a closer look within yourself — being honest, can you truly say that you live up to the standards and/or moral fiber that you profess to believe? Do you truly live up to that each time an instance comes along, or do you hedge and make excuses for why, this time, you did not? Wouldn't it just be more prudent, efficient, and honorable to do it right in the first place instead of making excuses for why you gave yourself an out this time? And isn't it true that if you are constantly giving yourself excuses and exceptions, then there is no real rule?

Integrity on a Daily Basis

We are not trying to make you feel bad, dear readers; we are simply pointing out that if you were all a little more like the butler in this story and honestly and truly lived up to what you know to be right and/or expected, wouldn't you all feel better about yourselves at the end of each day? Wouldn't you all feel better about yourselves at the end of your lives? Yes, we think the answer is obvious — of course you would! In this discourse, and indubitably in the entire book, we want people to think about what real integrity is and what it means on a daily basis.

We really do not think that this is something that is too hard to do each day. Just start by making it a good habit — an "act of will" to see and be in the integrity of each moment of your day. It's not that hard when you really think about it, but it is something that you might have to focus on more intently at first in order to make a change. Then just do that every day, and soon you will find that you are indeed becoming a person of substance, quality, and high integrity.

Integrity within Self: Attitudes and Belief Systems

In the story of the butler, he inherently knew and acted on this every day of his life, and people greatly admired him for it. His employer, the lord of the manor, had hired and kept him for that very reason. And in the end, we think his fellow employees respected him more for it too, even though they had complained a bit. They may not have agreed with him on his decision, but they knew and respected his reasons for it.

What about the butler's attitudes and belief systems? Did he not carry within himself the belief that all things were worth more and came together more when certain standards were upheld on a daily basis? He carried within himself the high standard of integrity that he expected of others. Long before idioms like "walking your talk" or "speaking your truth" became popular, the butler was doing and living these things.

When the lord first hired this butler many years before, the reason he hired him above the other candidates for the job was that the lord saw and sensed in him a greatness, a pure quality — an energy, if you will, that made him stand out over the others. The lord of the manor intuited that he could leave his estate in the hands of this man who, unbeknown to him at the time, had never been in charge of such a large estate or staff. Now, we are not suggesting that every person be hired in this manner, but in the case of this man, this butler, it was warranted in the extreme. Not only did he have the integrity and the wherewithal to do a good job, but he also had an undergirding of love, truth, and grace to be the best at whatever job he was placed in at any given time. A highly advanced soul, he cared about and for the great estate as if it were his own, sticking to the qualities and standards he expected of others.

His was an easy grace. He had a likeable but forthright manner about him that exuded a positive, cooperative energy, and he was approachable and easy to work with. He had a knack of being able to figure out any problem — nothing seemed too hard for him. His staff, for the most part, enjoyed working with him, and not only was his reputation stellar, but it was greatly enhanced by his ability to work well with others and to get the best out of them in the most loving, caring, and respectful way possible. The lord of the manor knew that he had a very special person at the helm of his ship.

The Butler's Youth: An Important Life Lesson

As for this butler's ability to concentrate and focus on the matter at hand, he had not always been good in this respect. In a prior job, he had a task to complete and had gotten distracted by a woman who worked there on the staff. The butler had been much, much younger, and this woman was very beautiful and alluring, and being the young man that he was, he "fell in love" with her — or so he thought. But it turned out that the woman was attracted to another, and he had been deeply wounded at the time. Later on, however, he realized that it had only been an infatuation.

What had happened was this: During the time the butler was being affected by the distraction of the woman, he had been in charge of cleaning a certain portion of a large house, and on a certain day when there were preparations for a great party, he forgot to clean the stairs — to check and clear them of any small debris that might be left over from dogs and children running up and down. So on this particular day the party commenced, one of the guests, a woman, went rushing up the stairs to tell the mistress something, and she tripped and fell down a small flight of stairs where a toy had been left. The butler had been so distracted by the other young woman that he had missed it. Luckily, the woman only slightly injured. She had barely turned her ankle and had some bruising, but he felt very bad about it, of course. The mistress forgave him, but he resolved then and there to never let a personal matter interfere with his job — and he never did again.

Diversity within Unity: Running a Large Estate

We want to talk about another aspect of our "diversity within unity" theme. In this particular story, we have a butler in charge of a large staff. Each member of the staff has their own particular duties and portions of the house to uphold and keep clean and tidy. The laundry is done daily, and particular care is taken in the washing, folding, putting away in drawers and hanging up in closets, and so forth. The kitchen staff obtains and prepares the food for the three daily meals for the lord of the manor and any family and friends staying there.

As mentioned before, there is a horse arena for which care and maintenance is required daily. The gardeners must take daily care of the grounds and surrounding gardens. The entire staff receives instructions daily, and the butler oversees everything and makes sure that every person and every job is in cooperation, concordance, and balance with the daily activities on any particular day. Special events, again, must be carefully and centrally organized and coordinated in order to have everything in preparation beforehand for big events.

There are a lot of different things that must be coordinated and synchronized for the daily running of such a large estate. Many diverse things must come together each day in cooperation and union with each other, must they not? The theme of diversity within unity is certainly present, and it is inherent in the layering and weaving of this story. The butler is the unifying factor within this parable, is he not? A large estate such as the one that he serves could not operate without an overseer of sorts, could it? He is the one responsible for directing the action on a daily basis, for without him, all might end up in chaos.

The Will of the Lord of the Manor: Divine Will

The many diverse duties all have a central far-reaching purpose and design. The purpose of the maintenance has coupled with the design, or will, of the lord of the manor. Therefore, all is taken care of and watched over as the lord desires.

In this case, the butler knows and embodies, if you will, the lord's desire. The lord's will has become the butler's will, and vice versa. So as we see here, the lord's will — divine will — has become the butler's will.

9

Arnold

Once there was a boy named Arnold. Arnold lived in an old shack down by a river bank near a creek called "the Waddy." He lived there with his parents who were so poor they had no money at all and continually lived hand to mouth. Every day was a struggle of survival for his parents. He had two sisters, Edna and Marie, who were grown and on their own, but Arnold had been an "oops" baby, as his mother had been forty-one and already in the change of life when she had him. At that time, many years ago, a woman in her forties having a child was considered almost scandalous, but here came little Arnold, named after his dad (but totally oblivious to that, of course). He was a good boy, and in spite of his parents' extreme poverty, they loved him very much.

Arnold was a delight to his parents as he went through all his baby and toddler stages. His mother and father just glowed with delight and love every time they saw him and as he went through his early childhood years. They were almost sorry to see him grow up. He was such a delightful child and the apple of their eye, and they spent whatever money they could scrape up on his well-being and welfare.

Arnold grew up and went to a little schoolhouse on the other side of the bayou where there was only one teacher for all the grades, but this teacher was very competent and did well with all her students. She especially liked Arnold. He was such a delight, an eager and avid learner. He did so well in his studies that by the time he had reached the end of sixth grade, he was already at the eighth grade level. His teacher did not know what to do, since Arnold was almost thirteen years old and was already academically ready for high school.

That summer Arnold's teacher talked to a teacher friend who had a friend in the nearest township. They in turn talked to the school board about allowing Arnold to go to a high school in town despite his young age. Arnold's teacher told the board how bright and smart he was, and they sent for him so that they could talk to him and his parents. His parents put on the best clothes they had — his mom put on the only nice dress and matching pair of shoes she had, and his dad wore an old suit. Arnold wore his best shirt and a pair of knickerbockers.

They went before the board of education to request an early entrance for Arnold. He felt that he was ready, and he was very mature for his age. He convinced the school board that he could handle it, and they agreed. The only problem seemed to be how to get him there every day, as his parents lived far out in a shack and had no money for gas to take him back and forth to town every day. So it was arranged that Arnold could live with his elementary school teacher, who had a house on the north side of town. She promised his parents that she would make sure he got to and from school every day. And so it was arranged.

At the end of the summer, Arnold's parents tearfully took him to town again, their hearts almost breaking, and left their precious boy with his teacher, Miss Annie. Miss Annie understood Arnold's parents' pain at leaving the only child they had left in the hands of a virtual stranger, but she reassured them that she cared about Arnold and his welfare and would take good care of him. She invited them to come and visit whenever they could. The parting was very painful for the parents, who were afraid they might never see their son again. They knew they were so poor that they could not afford to visit him very often, if at all, but their only salve was the fact that he loved his teacher, Miss Annie — and that he loved to learn. While he had gone through the different grades in that little schoolhouse on the bayou, Arnold could never get enough of reading books. When the other children were at recess, he was always still inside reading a book. He just couldn't get enough of learning, and Miss Annie knew this, which is why she fought so hard for him to go to high school early. She knew he could handle it, and she knew that, in spite of his youth, he would do well. And he did. He made an easy adjustment to high school and soon was amazing both the students and faculty with his intelligence and wit. He became known as "Arnold the Boy Wonder," and he graduated at age sixteen at the top of his graduating class!

Arnold's parents were so proud of him. They sat at his graduation in awe and wonder of what their boy had accomplished. There were tears of joy, and his mother wept when she hugged him. They went over to thank Miss Annie for her help over the past few years, and they told her that they could not have provided the kind of life and opportunities for him that she had. They had only been to see him once or twice a year after he had moved in with Miss Annie, as they were still as poor as church mice. Arnold's father, unbeknown to Arnold, was suffering from a serious illness and was not expected to live out the year, but he and his wife did not tell Arnold so that he could concentrate on getting into a good college. He had had a lot of offers for scholarships to some of the best colleges in the country. Miss Annie advised him to take the one offered by Yale, so he did. Miss Annie also helped him move to Connecticut so he could start the new fall semester there.

Arnold became a bit noteworthy in the local area once the news got out that one of Yale's incoming freshmen was a sixteen-year-old from the bayous of Louisiana who had grown up in poverty in a shack. After that, every time he accomplished some major achievement or became a student adjunct, it would be in the paper as "Arnold the Boy Wonder Does It Again!" and so on. He had become newsworthy.

In the middle of his freshman year, Arnold got word that his father had died, and he took a week off to go back to Louisiana for the funeral. It was a simple funeral, paid for by Miss Annie, who had befriended Arnold's parents. She invited his mother to come and live with her, since life was hard on the bayou. Arnold's mother consented only because she too was getting a little infirm due to her hard life and an accident had left her partially crippled in one leg. So, reluctantly at first, she moved in with Miss Annie in town, and they eventually grew very close.

Arnold continued his upward climb in college and graduated cum laude from Yale at age twenty. Of course, the papers were right there reporting on his graduation — "20 Year-Old Boy Wonder Graduates Cum Laude from Yale — Job Offers Galore!" was the headline.

Of course, Miss Annie and his mother were there at his graduation. Both of them just could not believe how much Arnold had accomplished in his short life. He too was proud and very happy. Now he had a chance to give his mother some things that he had wanted to for a long time: a big beautiful house to live in, nice clothes, and a new car.

He became an engineer at one of the preeminent upcoming aeronautics and manufacturing companies. They offered him a generous salary for that day and time, and within two years Arnold bought his mother a magnificent old Southern mansion in the town where Miss Annie lived and he had gone to high school. His mother invited Miss Annie to come and live in the "new" house; they had become like sisters and were very close. Arnold came to visit them occasionally on weekends and holidays, and they all had a wonderful life, thanks to the little boy, Arnold, who started with nothing, but became something — something wonderful!

10

Oscar

Otters are always thought of as furry, fuzzy, and cute creatures of lakes, streams, and oceans, and so they are, but they are also very resourceful, intelligent creatures whose ability to float on the water for most of their lives is uncanny and unique. Hardy and playful, they are able to quickly make adjustments to whatever habitat they find themselves in.

We will follow the story of a fellow named Oscar. He was quite a clever fellow, and as he grew up, he loved to play in the ponds of his home area. Sleek and quick, he found he could swim faster and farther than the others. He was very adventurous and a bit mischievous and foolhardy, this Oscar.

One day he swam very far out and down the river that flowed from this pond, and he got caught up in the strong current. On and on it swept him until he heard a sound that was strange and unfamiliar to him — waves crashing! He struggled to get to the side of the river, and as the water swirled around him, he saw a group of rocks to the right. Adept and strong, he leaped for the rocks and quickly found himself inside an underwater cavern.

The lights in this cave were very beautiful, unlike anything Oscar had ever seen before. The scene before him was very different from where he had grown up. His home pond and river had always been bathed in sunlight, and the river was always full, with enough fish for all. No one had ever gone this far down the river, as far as he knew.

The mysterious beauty of the cave enthralled him. He swam around easily and just laid on his back for a long time watching the exquisite scene. Then he thought he saw movement out of the corner of his eye. A very large dolphin had swiftly and silently entered the cave. Suddenly there were many dolphins, coming from somewhere underneath the cavern walls. As they surfaced, one of them rose up on his great tail and spoke:

"Brother otter, we bring greetings and welcome to you this day. You were not aware of it, but we brought you here to speak to you about a matter of great importance. We of the Dolphin Clan wanted to inform you and your family about some things that are about to happen on our planet. Now, we don't want you and your family to be alarmed, but our beautiful planet is about to make some changes that she needs to make, and she will be moving things around a bit. You and your clan will be all right, however, and we are bringing this message to you as a way of informing as many of the clans as we can of the coming changes. As guardians of the great oceans along with our whale brothers, we have known that the Great Mother was going to have to move around a bit. What we would like you to do is to go back and tell as many as you can what is going to happen and not to worry. When the planet starts moving, you and your family will be taken care of and shown what to do and where to go. We know that the Otter Clan in particular is very good at adapting to change, and that your family can help the other animal clans when the time comes. We will stay in communication with you — you will hear my voice in your thoughts and mind giving you instructions on where to go, when, and so on. Please tell the others not to be afraid, and that we will all ride this out together."

Oscar was astonished to hear the dolphin speaking to him. He seldom spoke, or was spoken to, by any of the other animals around him when he was growing up. He had enjoyed playing by himself and with his fellow otters in the peaceful surroundings of his childhood, and they had had many fun-filled adventures. And now this very important dolphin, obviously the leader, was speaking to him about strange things to come.

"I am honored that you would speak to me," Oscar said, "but why are these things happening? What is happening to our world? Is something wrong? Is something bad going to happen? You're frightening me!"

The dolphin was about to speak again when Oscar saw one of the other dolphins calmly and slowly rise up out of the water and, as though winking, she caught his eye. She sent Oscar a telepathic message that he was not to worry — that they would be protected from any harm. Her kind eyes and reassuring manner calmed him, and he listened as the great dolphin continued on.

"All of our Earth Mother's pinions and sinews must be stretched ever so slightly for a certain period of time," said the dolphin leader. "No one knows how long that time will be, but we know that it is a natural process called a 'water cycle,' and in this cycle our Great Mother, who has been in great imbalance and disharmony, must bring herself back into a place of balance and homeostasis in order to continue being our home, the nest for all of us that she so lovingly and willingly supports. It is part of her cycle of change, and it is the way that this can be accomplished. For her, it is a small stretch here and there, but for us here on the surface and inhabiting the seas, it will feel like a lot.

"We know that many may react in fear at first, but we, the guardians of the great oceans, will see to it that as many of you as possible are moved or can be moved to safer areas while she must be 'in travail,' so to speak. She herself has assured us that what is happening is not a bad thing nor anyone's fault, but that it is just time — time for her to get herself back into balance, homeostasis, and harmony, maintaining the great symbioses of all life — the unity that she usually and easily sustains. We of the Dolphin Clan are here to help all of you in any way we can. Please try not to be afraid — we are with you all!"

And with a great flick of his tail, the dolphin disappeared under the water as he and his pod swam away.

Oscar was quite dismayed at hearing about what was about to happen, but he also felt a calm reassurance from all of the dolphins that everything was going to be okay. At that moment he doubted that this would be so, but he also had faith in the manner in which the message had been delivered. He felt strengthened and reassured. And they *had* said that his family and all the other families would be informed and taken care of when the time came.

"After all," he thought, "we otters *are* very intelligent and adaptable creatures — we can do it! We can tell all the others where to go and when, when the time comes. I must hurry back!" He found his way out of the cave and scurried back up the riverbank until he came to his home. What a journey he had had that day!

Later that day, Oscar needed to sort things out in his mind, to try to make sense of the extraordinary events of the day. So he started dialoguing to himself, saying, "Whoa … did that dolphin actually talk to me? Why would he want to talk to me? Wait, wait … I think I'm hearing something. Oh, wait … wait … I think I hear his voice again."

"Yes, you are hearing me again, Oscar," the Great Dolphin said. "I am speaking to you in your head. It is the way we of the Dolphin Clan have talked to others for a long time. Do not be alarmed. You're not going crazy. It's just that when we need to contact you about anything, this is the easiest and best way to do it. Creating that first meeting with you, Oscar, was not easy to do. Now, we did not make the river go faster, but we waited until it did, and then we kind of helped you along and kept you in the strong current, and then you did the rest. We were hoping that you could find the sacred grotto, and we just got lucky!

"We saw you bolt from the river just in time to avoid the crashing waves, as they are called. Your otter cousins, the sea otters, are adept with crashing waves, but we know that you are not used to them. And Oscar, because we knew how clever and smart you are, you swam around under water and found the only entrance to the cave — and it was under water! So, Oscar, do not be afraid of this way of communicating."

"But," Oscar responded, "I've never been able to speak this way before. How can I hear you now?"

"We helped you, dear Oscar. We opened your inner ears, so do not be afraid. You will get used to it and to hearing my voice. Remember, we're with you when you need us!"

Oscar shook his head back and forth as if to clear it. He had to think about this some more. "I wonder what this is called." He thought the dolphins had gone away.

"This is called mental telepathy, and it is something that used to be used on Earth many, many ages ago but is now a lost art. Please understand, you are *not* going crazy! I heard your question. Now, I'm not listening in all the time, Oscar. You have the privacy of your own thoughts, but somehow I was alerted to your question, like a phone ringing, okay?" Remember, dear readers, this is our fable, and in it, otters know what a phone is.

"Okay," said Oscar. "I think I understand better now." And with that he lay around in the pools of the river and ate fish for dinner.

Now, our Oscar was an interesting fellow, even for an otter. Blessed with high intelligence, he had always been a very curious guy when he was little. And oftentimes he would get into little scrapes and mishaps. One time he had an encounter with a large bird and her nest. He had discovered it on the ground by a marshy area, but just when he peered over to see what was in it, the mother bird attacked him from behind, nipping him and loudly squawking at him, raising her large wings up and down — it was quite a comical scene! With a bruised ego but basically uninjured — and most certainly duly chastised — he had made a hasty retreat back to his mama.

So our young intrepid warrior had grown up with an appreciation for the world at large around him, more than the others. And so that day he had gone way far out on the large river, exploring, playing, and as always, looking for food for the day. That's how he had gotten caught in the main current of the river. Oscar knew he had gone a little too far.

However, sometimes life will place someone like our otter friend in an unusual situation that can be very compelling, pulling them this way and that to see how they handle it. Do they panic and react with fear, or do they go with it and try to see the other possibilities that exist within the framework of that moment, within that unexpected situation that could be fraught with potentiality and purpose?

Which will it be today? Could you be a little like our otter friend, Oscar, and "go with it"? Could he have rendezvoused with our dolphin friends had he not found a way to survive, to turn around a situation just bursting with different possibilities and have the courage to find the magic in the moment? And what could that moment possibly be? Magic or disaster?

And so our beloved otter Oscar was faced with quite an important and interesting responsibility and dilemma, one he was not sure he could complete. He had been very moved by the words from the dolphin but was still in tremendous wonderment and curiosity about the specific meaning of the words. He had felt their import and sensed the great quickening of Earth that was going to happen, but he was no longer in fear. The dolphins had been able to impart a deep recognition of the importance and gravity of what was going to happen along with an unusual feeling of peace and acceptance. He felt no fear anymore. Indeed, he felt very brave and smart, with a newfound confidence that even he had not experienced in his life before. He knew with intense certainty that he could do it. He didn't quite know how it was all going to play out or when exactly, but an inner knowing told him to stay calm, centered — if an otter can feel centered — and focused. He was a new "otter-man"!

Later that day, Oscar laid on his back in the water, pondering many things (remember, this is a fairy story, so otters can ponder). "Who are my people — my clan? Are the dolphins part of my clan? And the other animals — are these my people too? Are they the ones to whom the Great Dolphin was referring? How can I find out who my family is? I don't know who to ask. You know what," he thought, "I'll go ask my mother if she knows what is meant by that."

So the next morning Oscar swam over to his mother's area in the eastern portion of the little lake and said, "Mother, who is in our clan? What is it about them that makes them part of our family?"

"Son," she replied, "I'm not sure why you are asking me this. It is fairly simple to discover. If you see the other otters who look like us, then they are our family. I'm not sure, really. We have so many cousins and aunts and grandfathers. I mean … you know, your brothers, Wilbur and Abel, and your sisters, Rebecca and Shirley. They, as you know, are in our immediate family, but I don't know everyone that is in our family. We're quite a large family — that's all I know. Did you have breakfast yet? Did you have your morning fish? There is quite a good area at the far end over there that always seems to have such tasty morsels. I'll see you later!" And off she swam. After all, she was a mother otter, and that's how she saw herself — no less, no more.

"But," Oscar thought to himself, "that didn't quite answer my question. How do I find this out? Who is my family?"

Instantly, he heard in his head a small voice, "We are your family." And he looked overhead and saw a flock of bluebirds flying by.

"And *we* are your family too!" he heard from behind him.

Swinging around, he noticed a pair of slugs oiling their way along the shore. "No," Oscar thought, "I didn't just hear them say that. That can't be … can snails talk to me?"

Then, as he continued to look in the same direction, he heard another voice, an odd one that seemed to be coming from the direction of some rocks lying nearby. "No," he thought. "Now I'm *really* hearing things!"

And the rock spoke again. "Hey, it's me — over here. You know, the funny-shaped rock with the moss all over it to your left. Yep, that's me — that's the one. And *yes*, I'm speaking to you!"

Incredulous, Oscar wiped his eyes, shook his head, and blinked a couple times in disbelief. "You're my family? Really? And your fellow rocks too?"

"Yes, yes, we all are. Don't be alarmed. It's just that we heard you ask the question and wanted to help you with the answer."

"How can *you* be my family? And how can the birds or the slugs be my family? Really — I didn't know. I've never asked that question before. Can you explain, please?"

Now, Oscar was a bright fellow who was always quick and resourceful in figuring out things, but this was an extremely perplexing new puzzle that he had never encountered before. Not the one that the dolphins had relayed — no, he felt fully assured and unafraid concerning that. No, it was this new problem that had come up in answer to his queries about family that he was concerned with. "How can this be?" he said to himself. "How can birds, common slugs, and even rocks be my family too? I mean, I can understand that they are my friends, but they are not of my clan. They don't look anything like an otter should. Look, my family hunts and eats fish; they swim, play, and lay around in the water of ponds, lakes, and small rivers; and I've heard some other clans even do this in that place where the water crashes a lot — in those waters. But there is *no way* that birds, slugs, or rocks could be my family! No way! I just don't see how!"

Just then, magically (this is a fable, correct?) Oscar heard a deep voice in his head say, very faintly at first, "Don't be afraid! It is me, the Great Dolphin of the grotto speaking. Yes, we are *all* family!"

Oscar blinked hard again, then rubbed his eyes and looked around, seeing no one. "Are you speaking to me? You sound like the dolphin in the cavern."

"Yes, it is me, for I'm the representative of the Dolphin Clan appointed to speak to you about many things. So in answer to your question, how can these others be your family, we can tell you most assuredly that they are *all* your family. Know that all the kingdoms and clans of the topside of our great seas are indeed, in a very real sense, your brothers and sisters. Of course, they don't seem like they could be, do they? But let's examine it for a moment. Of course, as you well know, they look different and communicate within their respective clans differently. Crabs and slugs most certainly don't move their bodies like you do, do they? In fact, crabs can sometimes look quite comical, with their eyes on stems and their ability to move sideways — it can be amazing! Or examine our lowly slug, sliming his way along the shore — an odd-looking fellow, to be sure. Or the great bird clans whose 'arms' developed the ability to fly through the oceans of air that surround our planet."

"How can these creatures be like us?" said Oscar. "You are right. We are all so very different. How can this be?"

The voice of the Great Dolphin grew still for a moment, and then he proceeded. "We are going to play a game. This game is called "Look and See." I will open up your eyes in a different way, friend otter, so that you can look inside each one of these creatures in a very special way. Now when you are ready, pretend in your mind that you are looking through a microscope with your eyes." (In our fable, otters know what microscopes are.) "Now peer deeply into one of these and tell me what you see."

So Oscar closed his eyes, looked over at the slug in the mire, and tried to see the creature in his mind's eye. At first, he saw nothing and was about to open his eyes, but then suddenly he saw something — he thought he saw the inside of the creature. He thought he saw a tiny heart beating, and oh — what was that? All at once, he saw little eyes looking back at him — not physical eyes, but the eyes of something else, something deeper, blinking curiously at him. He looked even deeper … oh! What was that? A tiny, tiny light bulb became visible, like a wheel of rainbows! He blinked really hard again and withdrew his eyes.

"Okay," Oscar thought, "I'm really seeing things! What the heck was that looking back at me? It looked like a pair of eyes looking back at me. I can't figure this out — it's like I was looking inside of him. Let me try looking into one of the birds flying overhead. Let me see if I can do that."

As he looked again, he was able to penetrate deep into the body of a bird even as she was in flight. "Whee! I get the feeling that I'm flying too," Oscar thought. "And what's that? I feel as if I'm seeing through her eyes. Why, there I am down there on the shore. That's me! I can see myself through her eyes. I could feel her heart beating for a minute there. How can this be? Are we more alike than different? *I* have eyes. *I* have a heartbeat. Hmm … I like this game. Let's look even deeper. Does she have that rainbow thing I saw in the slug? Let's see!"

As soon as he thought this, Oscar's inner eyes saw even deeper into the bird than before. Suddenly again he saw the brilliant blazing of many colors, like tiny prisms of light all around, dazzling his inner vision. Startled, he pulled his vision out of the bird.

Puzzled, he again addressed the voice of the dolphin. "This is a very strange game. How am I able to see these things? I've never been able to see like that before. What did you do to me?"

The great voice replied, "I didn't really do anything to you. I merely gave you the ability to see as we of the Dolphin Clan see. We see everything in this way. It is how we know that we are all more alike than we are different. Each clan, each life form, has expressed the life and inner light in a different outward garb — the forms that we all see with our physical eyes. But our inner eye, which I opened up for you, pierces into the deeper, subtler life that is going on beneath and within the outer garb. Deep within lie smaller and smaller pieces of all of us. The inner eye can perceive what our physical eyes cannot. Yet those things that you saw were always there. And those things, at their deepest level, are nothing more than light and life itself in all its tiny, beautiful majesty, there for anyone to see if they dare to look close enough. Now, brother otter, take these same eyes and look within yourself for a moment. Remember, it's a game, and otters like games, so humor me. Take a closer look."

Oscar closed his eyes again and focused his eyes inwardly, back behind his physical eyes for a moment. Deeper and deeper he went. Then, as if in a dream, he saw something very unusual, something he did not expect to see: tiny sparkling rainbow prisms suddenly burst upon his inner sight! And everywhere he turned his focus, there they were — they were everywhere inside of him! Startled, he jumped out of the inner vision and opened his eyes. "What is this, some kind of trick? How come I am seeing the lights inside of me too? How can this be?"

Calmly, the voice answered back, "Because you and we are all made of the same basic components of life and light. All of those tiny light bulbs inside of you are in everything. Yes, you are an otter, and yes, he is a slug, but deep inside we are all members of this planet made of the same building blocks — looking through the same eyes, beating the same hearts. The secret is that most beings do not know it — but *we* know the truth, and now, you do too! All we did was open up your deeper inner eye to see what is already there. It is there in all of us, all the clans and all of the kingdoms. We are more alike than we are different — you saw it for yourself."

Oscar began shaking his head as if to clear it. "Are you sure that my mind is not just making this up? Am I dreaming, or am I really seeing these things and hearing your words?"

"Remember, friend otter, that I told you that I would be there for you, to give you guidance and instruction when the time came. Well, when you asked the question of who your family was, we thought that giving you this additional information would help you to move everybody when the time comes. That way, you too will better understand that when we said your family would be all right and taken care of, we meant not just your otter clan, but *all* the clans, all the kingdoms of the land.

"We will be telepathically sending messages to you, and you will give them to whoever is next in line from you. Then they will send the message on down the line, so to speak — like a relay — until all are informed and in readiness. Then, with certain signals, all will be prepared when our Mother Earth needs to move and will do what is necessary when the time comes. Again, we felt that you needed to see and hear for yourself who your family is. Do you understand better now?"

"Yes, I do," replied Oscar. "Yes, I really think I do now. Thank you."

"All right then. We will talk again soon." And the dolphin voice stopped as suddenly as when he had first heard it.

Oscar carefully looked around him in wonder at the new information given to him. "Wow! So it's true then that we are all so connected. I never had really thought about it before. I just thought that all of us were so different. I didn't know that inside we are all so alike. I saw it with my own eyes. I felt it inside of me. Say, I *saw* the inside of me! I never knew this inner world even existed, but it was right there in front of me the whole time! Wow!"

Our good friend, Oscar, was a little perturbed and startled by what had just happened to him. He lay around in quiet pools of water later that day, just pondering it for a long time. He was very intrigued by what he had been able to see, but had as yet been unable to put it fully into a perspective that, as an otter, he could understand. He understood at least partly that the other creatures and he were, after all, creatures together. But what about all of the light that he saw? What exactly was he looking at? There were pretty lights, but … So Oscar was lying on his back contemplating everything. And since, after all, this *is* a parable, let's go into his brain and help him, shall we? He has figured out the basics of what he experienced, but now we're going to dialogue with him in his head:

So, Oscar, do you have anything that you're wondering about, or do you have a question or a comment? Let's talk.

[Looking around again] Who is this? Who are you? Are you the dolphin again?

No. We're the "answerers of questions." Can we help you?

Well, I was a bit confused by the rainbow lights. What was that all about? Why were they so tiny? It seemed like they were everywhere. What are they, exactly?

We're going to give you an answer within another answer — sort of a riddle. You are the light.

I'm the light? What do you mean?

We mean that light is energy, and light is what is in between, and part of, the smallest particles of your being — you. You see, the real part of you is not strictly physical. It's not what is called physical matter. Light is what is in between the atoms, cells, and molecules of your body. You can't see yourself in between these tiniest of particles — and we mean really, really tiny, except that you will see it as light.

Oh wow! Really? You mean all that light was the real me?

Yes, something like that. There's more to it than that, of course, but it is the basic component of what we are talking about. All creation — everybody, everything, including rocks, mind you — has this light. It is what makes everything so alive!

Okay, wait a minute — did you just say that rocks have life too?

Yes — really! Oh, it is more of what we would call consciousness, which means that everything has its own awareness of a sort. And of course a rock's awareness would not be like yours, would it? But just as you are conscious and aware as an otter, rocks are aware, too, but in a very different way — wouldn't they be? A rock might feel very heavy or very magnetic, or very deep, might it not? Or it might sense itself as very porous, brittle, hard and very, very old.

I've never really thought about this before. Hmm … maybe.

Oh, more than maybe — for real. Absolutely for real!

So let me see if I understand you correctly. Rocks and I both have this light, this awareness, this … consciousness, did you say? But it expresses itself in so many ways. But on the inside part, the tiniest parts of all of us, we are alike. Is that right? *(We told you he was smart!)*

Yes, that's right. Very basic and simplistic, but basically that's right.

So is that what you and the dolphins meant by "we're all family"?

[Jumping up and down inside Oscar's head] Yes, yes! That's it — you got it! You got it! [Exiting his head.]

Oh, oh, okay. Okay. Yes, I guess I *do* understand it now. Weird — weird to think that rocks are my family. It's kind of weird, too, that that slug over there is my family too. Say, I wonder if that's why I saw two little eyes — his inner eyes — looking at me at one point. I wondered about that. Oh, wow, do I have a lot to think about now! But I'm happy. I got lots of answers to my questions. I guess it's a good day after all!

Oscar's Awakening

So here we have our cute otter, Oscar. And he has been having quite an awakening, hasn't he, dear reader? What conclusions can we draw so far with this story? Our little Oscar is having quite an adventure, isn't he? Let's summarize our story.

Our otter friend gets caught in a strong current of a river, which takes him to a clandestine but important meeting with the dolphins, who besides being the ocean guardians with their brothers, the whales, are actually in a broader capacity watching out for the welfare of the whole planet. Then they enlist Oscar to help and assist them in this endeavor. And in order to help him in that capacity, they give him a few extraordinary gifts to help him better understand not only the role he will play, but the reasons why.

They opened up his mind to hear them actually speaking. They created a pathway to his brain so he could hear them telepathically. They also helped open up not only his third eye, but an inner microscopic/telescopic eye that is a common occurrence in higher, subtler vibratory realms. The ability to see inwardly is a gift. It is an ability that the cetaceans of our world have naturally, along with their many other gifts, such as sonar. These are only a few of the many highly tuned abilities that are within their physical and vibratory range.

So they gifted our little otter, Oscar, with his own inner sight, and being the intelligent, curious, and readily adaptable fellow he was, he just went with it and found that a new world opened up to him. And to his surprise, it felt natural and normal to begin to see that way. He learned very quickly that his concept of family had expanded a bit, hadn't it?

How would *we* react if we could see like that too? Can you imagine it in your mind, dear reader? What do you think *you* could see? What new vistas would open up in front of your very eyes? And what new perceptions and insights would they hold? How would that change the way we look at things, how we currently view our world? What would you, dear reader, envision for your future — or ours — to see such a fascinating new inner world open up like that? Why, it would almost be like when microscopes were first invented in the 1600s. Scientists around the world could then see what had been there all the time — a little like cleaning a dirty window only to peer inside to see the treasures within. How fascinating! How eye-opening! How mind-blowing that would be! Doesn't it just delight the imagination? And the most interesting part is that it was there the whole time. Whew! I guess Oscar — and we too, perhaps — was missing a lot. There was a lot he didn't know!

Finding Your Own Inner Truth

At this point in our storyline, it has almost become superfluous how the story played out in the end. A little bit like the *Bhagavad Gita*, that great Eastern work; the main part of that story entailed the wisdoms that Krishna was able to impart to Arjuna, didn't it? It wasn't truly about the battle that did finally come; it was about what Arjuna learned about himself, wasn't it? His inner personal revelations and personal discoveries of self were the core of that story. The battle in the story was anticlimactic to the main thrust of Arjuna's inward battle with himself. Krishna merely dialogued with him and guided him, in a very eloquent manner, into finding his own inner truth, did he not?

And so it is, too, with our story of Oscar the otter, his new dolphin friends, and what exciting inner vistas he discovers along the way. Oscar's open mind, curious nature, and forthright, brave, and stalwart heart put him in good stead to make a quantum leap forward — especially for an otter! He trusted his heart and feelings to guide him — not by disconnecting his intellect, but by using the two in conjunction with each other. When the heart and mind work together synergistically and harmoniously, a great new "third energy" is created — a place where miracles can happen. It is a space, a place, a new energy balancing of the creative force, galvanizing, informing, and driving true creation and change. It is the fulcrum, the pivoting place where both worlds — inner and outer — can meet and where, having a greater understanding of each other, knowledge and transformation can occur. It is a powerful and wonderful thing to unite heart and mind, inner and outer, wisdom and communication with love — that is what our dear little Oscar was able to do — using all of those things to create and implement a better understanding of potentialities and solutions. He's quite a guy, our Oscar, and we are so proud of him!

The cetaceans, the dolphins, and the whales in our fable are considered to be the ocean guardians. Let us more closely define what we mean by explaining the history that whales and dolphins have together on our planet.

Whales, Dolphins, and the Seventh-Dimensional Highway

In our story, there is a legend that the whales and dolphins actually swam over to Earth from another planet very far away. In this legend, theirs was an ocean planet a lot like ours. On their world, they were both part of what we would call a spiritually evolved civilization in which the cetaceans, as they are called here, actually were sentient beings who walked on dry land with two legs. Because of their advanced telepathic and telekinetic abilities, they were able to discern and know about the evolution of our Earth.

As they saw us in our planet's earlier evolution millions of years ago, they decided to seed our oceans with their presence, both on land and in our oceans, to allow and assist the developing life here. Partly because of their advanced sonar/echoing abilities, partly because of our flora and fauna's inability to utilize oxygen at that time in Earth's history, and largely due to the tremendous amount of volcanic gases and ash, they decided to "swim" over to Earth by way of a seventh-dimensional highway they created called the Gateway of the Heavens that would bring them faster than the speed of light, like a ribbon "bowing" over from their planet to ours. This was done approximately 91 million years ago, according to the legend.

As the whales started to seed our oceans, singing and sounding their songs, it helped our oceans to stabilize and balance of the life force, and it helped create a better, more life-sustaining ocean environment for all life in the oceans of Earth at that time. The whales came first, and the land dolphins came much, much later. So whales and their cousins — the narwhals, the belugas, and their various related species — became implanted in Earth's oceans and coastal areas, and became part of the evolution of Earth history. The walking dolphins, when they did come — by virtue of their high intelligence, knowledge, and advanced abilities — agreed to help out on the land that was still continuing to sink and emerge. The whales, being from their planet, were also highly evolved creatures, and once they had stabilized Earth's oceans, they agreed to carry Earth's history through the ages in their genetic blueprint. As a result, anyone wishing to know Earth's history could connect with the whales to know our past.

According to the legend, the dolphins, through a series of unforeseen events, decided that they needed to be in the oceans and no longer be land creatures. So because of their advanced evolutionary capabilities, they were able to evolve themselves into our oceans over a long period of time .

Legend or Fact?

Now, as with any story, there comes a time when this legend must combine with the real story of Earth, and what we have just told you *is* the real story of how the cetaceans came to be here on this planet. If they could talk, they would tell you for themselves that the story related here is an accurate one. Although to many of you, dear readers, this may seem like it couldn't possibly be true, we assure you that it is actually *not* a fable, but the true history of the cetaceans' journey on this Earth. And they would like you to also know that they are returning to their home planet for a number of years, necessitated by the fact that Earth's history is now about to change and develop forward into the new millennium with a mighty leap — not in a drastic or bad way, but it will definitely be a change from what has been known and done here before.

This new millennium, contrary to the present temporary conditions, is in the process of a quantum leap forward in evolution, collectively creating a new collaboration as we all move forward in what will be a momentous movement unparalleled in the universe. The whales will return when it is the right time for them and us to be together again. Certain of their numbers will be staying behind to help keep our oceans alive and reasonably well until their return.

Concluding Oscar's Story

In concluding our otter story: Our dear little Oscar did his best. When the signal came through, he was able to hear the Great Dolphin's voice in his head and relay the needed and necessary information on down the line, so to speak, and all went very well. He never again questioned who his real family was, because he now knew the truth of the matter.

So as you all know by now, we want you to understand fully the meaning behind this magnificent story. Our little Oscar the otter learned quite a bit, didn't he? We wanted to point out a bit more of an overview and try to anticipate questions that our readers might have.

You see, the main thrust of this entire book is not only for you to enjoy the stories and "get" them for the different aspects of the law of one that each brings, but we want to make sure that you understand the overview of each one and how it relates to the whole — to both the entire book and to the whole of the concept of the law of one.

The Doppler Effect — A Further Look

We have anticipated that many of our readers may not quite understand features in this story, such as what the Doppler effect is. We know many of you are indeed familiar with this, as it is part of your daily weather forecasts, but we are going to speak here to those of you around the world who do not have access to television or watch at all.

So here is what we are talking about: When you stand on the shore and look out to sea, as you are looking way out past the horizon, we want you to think of a radio beam echoing in all directions from a central point. In this instance, instead of a radio tower atop a ship, we are going to have you stand on the beach and imagine that there's a whale out there — not too far, though — who is sounding an echo that goes out in concentric circles from the whale, out to the area of the sea that she inhabits. Then we want you to visualize her as she travels the great distances that she does, echoing in various places as she goes. Later she will have baby whales she will teach to do the same thing. Now, this echoing ability comes from a place in the whale's head, but it is propelled from the rest of its body with great force, like a loudly ringing bell. These echoes help the ocean vibrationally and energetically by sensing and giving it what it is lacking in order to maintain the delicate balance needed each season.

So when you are standing on a shore, think of what the whales do for all of us. They are doing quite a large service for our Mother Earth, so be sure to thank them for it. They do, indeed, hear and receive the prayers that we send, and in that way we can all communicate, support, and love each other in defense of, and love for, our beautiful planet. We want to thank you, dear readers, for being involved in our beautiful little story of Oscar the otter and how he and his cetacean friends saved Earth!

As you know, Oscar and the otter kingdom were picked to represent the land animals in our fable. Please understand, dear readers, that this doesn't elevate otters over other species or in any way denigrate the sanctity of the others. An otter was merely picked for the reason that it is an air-breathing land animal that spends most of its life in the water — that is why an otter was chosen for the task of representation in the story. Otters also have a very inquisitive nature and are highly intelligent creatures.

Of course, many other species, such as elephants, gorillas, orangutans, and others, are highly intelligent and somewhat adaptive, but you see, we couldn't have an elephant meet the Great Dolphin in the grotto, could we? Of course not! So you can all see one of the many reasons this particular fable had an otter as the protagonist. Do you see? All right.

We know many of you are animal lovers and probably wondered why we did not use one of your favorite animals. Of course, dear readers, these fables are representations only — that is why they are called fables and parables. The *context* of each story is what is important, not so much the structure that holds it.

We want to assure our readers that each and every animal on this planet — and ours too, for that matter — is special, unique, and important in and of its own right, and each helps to hold the balance and symbiosis of the planet. We just wanted to clarify this for everyone.

Each and every one of you is special, unique, and important too — and most of all, loved!

11

The Guardians

This story begins long ago, when the planet was much younger. Birds were still new to Earth then, and we find that they were, in many ways, still trying to find the best habitats for themselves and their families. The family of owls was very unusual — they were guardians of the land, and they were able to communicate with the whales and the dolphins, the guardians of the great seas of Earth.

Going back even further in time, the birds evolved from a dinosaur clan that mutated and branched off. Little feathers had started appearing on the hatchlings. Those feathers grew longer and stronger and slowly, very slowly, started replacing the reptilian wings with true feathers sturdy enough to achieve and maintain flight. One particularly hardy bunch of hatchlings was very brave and adventurous and would jump from their nests. In that falling, the first "real bird" spread his wings and, lo and behold, the first flight happened! Soaring over his brothers and sisters, he bravely shouted in glee, for the glory of true flight had begun!

Soon all of the little ones learned to achieve this tremendous feat. Before long, the other species of birds that were then appearing on the planet began inexplicably to fly, including the entire Owl Clan (the 100th monkey effect). Over time they developed very large and powerful wings and became masters of flight. As their large wings were developing, they still walked on the ground. The other bird species noticed their power, beauty, and high intelligence, and they became leaders in the bird community.

Now, in this fable, dolphins are land creatures that have started to evolve themselves to the seas, and they had long observed the owls' evolutionary progression. One day the dolphins approached an older owl with these words: "We notice that you are held in high esteem and regard by all the other bird kingdoms. And even the land creatures have begun to look to you for information, wisdom, and guidance. So we want to ask you if you would consider being the guardians of the lands of this great planet. Would you consider it?"

And the old, wise owl replied, "I must first ask the Great Council of Owls. I will let you know in a fortnight. Thank you for this great honor." And so he went before the high council and, after much discussion, the Owl Clans decided to accept. They accepted being guardians on the basis that if, after a trial period of 1,000 years, they still wanted it and felt able to do it, then they would become the permanent guardians.

And so at first everything went fine. They stayed in communication with the dolphins and whales and all was well. But as many years went by, the owls started encountering some problems. Because, you see, as one became a land guardian, one had to learn many things and undergo certain specific training for each area of the Earth. The forests of Earth required certain energies and tasks to be performed, and being watched over on a regular basis to maintain the delicate balance and perfection necessary.

At first the owls were excited and performed their tasks around the world very well, but as generations went by, gradually the younger owls started forgetting their duties or not really caring to do them. So the Planetary Hierarchy met to discuss what to do, because all of the Earth systems and ecosystems still needed tending and needed certain things to be done for them to maintain life on the planet. It was decided that they had to find another land guardian. This was not easy, and they asked the owls to continue doing as much as they could until another group of guardians could be found. After much searching, a substitute was found. A certain species was evolving that looked promising, but it looked like it was going to take a while. In the meantime, training started within the members of the devic realms, who were asked if they could expand their roles and take over for a time while the others got to the point of maturity at which training could commence. So they agreed to take over on a temporary basis.

So the owls were slowly released from their duties and obligations, and eventually they went back to just being owls again. But a few of them still retained the old knowledge and passed it down in an attempt to still help out Earth in some small way if it ever needed it. And occasionally the deva would indeed ask for their help during crises. The few who retained the old knowledge would spring forth to help out the world in times of great need. Trustworthy and forthright, these few noble owls kept their old legacy and promise alive and made the owls proud again!

And so it was that the owls were very important to Earth for a time when the planet was young, when the continents were still forming and oceans were heaving, foaming, and finding the low-lying basins of the Earth to lie upon. At first the owls had done so very well with their new tasks and duties. The call had gone out to all the owl clans to learn the new energies and how to apply them to keep the fauna and flora on Earth balanced and energized, making sure that each plant and animal spirit (remember, this is a fairy story) kept the divine design, the DNA, of each creation in perfection, beautiful and balanced.

So the owls learned how to oversee all of the other kingdoms around the Earth with a system of checks and balances, and how to coordinate everything according to the ocean guardians' directions and specifications. The animal and plant kingdoms worked well with, and under, the owls' jurisdictions, and all was balanced and kept in perfect harmony for a long period of time.

Now, this is not to say that Earth changes were not happening — because they were — but the owls had been taught how to coordinate the energies of all the systems and kingdoms on a daily basis. So as things were in constant flux, these checks and balances kept track of all of it as they moved and stretched, changed and settled back again. All was still in balance, and the owls maintained the oneness, divine design, and order as they went.

The owl clans did a very good job for a very long time, as we have said, and no one was sure when the break occurred. The owl clans taught all the young owlets when they reached a certain age and maturity, and the great guardian traditions were handed down from generation to generation. With great honor and ceremony, and as each owlet learned the ropes, they were deemed ready to assume the duties and protocols of each of their territories. And for a long time, they did very well.

Now, the owls had their turn at being guardians, but what happened was that at some point over many years and many generations, one of the teachers among the owls started to falter. This particular owl, through no fault of his own and unbeknown to him at the time, began using a teaching method that was slightly off. It began because he was in an area that had a tremendous slippage underground. What happened changed the harmonics and magnetics of this particular area, so when this owl toned the balancing of the energies one day, the harmonics were off ever so slightly, and the young owlets who were in training and who toned with him did not know of it. So this part of the guardian training was passed down incorrectly that year. And because the melodies were slightly off, this gradually started to weaken whole regions of Earth. By the time the problem was discovered, there was a weakness in the grid. By then so many owls were involved that plans had to be made to strengthen the grid quickly. That's when the members of the devic realms agreed to step in and reinforce it so that all species and all life in the affected regions could continue as before. The majority of the owls relinquished guardianship, as the other kingdoms took over for a time. And all was well again.

, , ,

The Living Grid of Earth

A side note here on the intricacies of the harmonic tones in regard to the living grid of Earth: It is the unity principle in a bitonal mode. Each area of Earth produces a certain tone or note that, along with other tones, comprises a beautiful but very intricate rainbow-like weaving of tones, each making its own harmonic chorus, if you will, for its particular area. Then the guardians enrich this by superintoning over these weavings what is needed for that particular year and area of Earth.

Whale Song: Symbiotic Interweaving

For instance, whale songs are intoned each year for the particular needs of that year, as the needs will vary from year to year. In this way, the intricate and beautiful rainbow-like harmonies keep everything in perfect balance at the exact time that it is needed for that certain area of the ocean. This toning replenishes the energies.

This is an intense oversimplification of a very complex interweaving of a symbiotic process. As the whales sing their songs, there is an echo and reverberation called the Doppler effect, which, when the whales do it, reverberates even into the rocks and bedrock of the earth itself, echoing to the core of the planet and back again. It is a very precise and delicate process that we have oversimplified, and it must be done synergetically and synergistically at regular intervals all around the globe.

The Doppler effect is one that is used by your scientists to keep track of aircraft and in your sonar equipment. It is also used by your weather people, the meteorologists, to track weather and the development of the progression of storms around the planet. In the larger scheme of things, it is also used by weather satellites around the globe for tracking the inception, velocity, and direction of hurricanes and storms producing tornadoes. But it is also used for tracking submarines and for underwater exploration in the oceans. A very sophisticated application of the Doppler effect through radar was essentially how the terrain at the bottom of the oceans was mapped. But whales and dolphins, the cetaceans, have been using it for millions of years in a very advanced and "medicinal" way to help keep the planet in balance. The very advanced sonar technologies used by whales and dolphins help the vibration of all life on the planet. Unseen and undetected healing and balancing frequencies accompany the sending out of the songs, tones, clickings, and so on that the whales and dolphins emit.

Keeping Earth in Balance

Unknown to scientists at this time is how the planet uses these frequencies and vibrations for food — for nourishment. The frequencies are sent out at regular intervals, replenishing the life energy of the planet as a whole and maintaining, interweaving, and bringing balance to the planet. The tones and frequencies they bring actually help keep the magnetics of Earth in balance by connecting with each other in an interdependent manner. As things are sometimes in flux and imbalances are created, these tonings refine and clear not only the atmosphere but all things.

Now we have told you all about what the whales do and what their contribution is to the planet. What we want to do here is this: There are any number of creatures on the planet that can help the whales to replenish the energies of the ocean each year. Surprisingly, jellyfish have a symbiotic relationship with the whales to pick up and re-resonate the sounds through their gelatinous body structures. Starfish, too, help bring in the energy and vibrations to the coastal areas of the world. Dolphins, of course, help carry and enhance the echoing, especially on the surface of the waters where they live. These very vibrations that the whales create — especially the great whales, who can sound at great depths beneath the waves — actually penetrate the bedrock and go down into and through the crust of the earth.

Remember, as we told you, rocks are not just "dead" like you think. They are, of course, very magnetic, but they are not as dead as you would think. Many of them have properties you might not think rocks would have, such as field magnetism, auric fields, and the ability to funnel life energy to name a few. Crystalline rocks are well known for their ability to hold and move light, energy, sound, and color, so when the whales are sounding and singing their beautiful songs, the very bedrock of the planet responds to and is benefitted by them. The waves of sound, energy, color, and vibration are able to reach great distances and depths, both on their own and with "a little help from their friends."

So we hope that all of you, dear readers, are seeing a pattern here. The entire Earth is one big, symbiotic ball orbiting in space. Let's remember that we are a part of those beautiful, intricately woven webs of symbioses and that we should work in harmony, balance, and unity with our mother Earth — not against her. Let's be part of the process and the solution, not part of the problem. And let's all remember, too, that our great strength lies in what we pull together — not in what we pull apart!

Returning to our story, our owl friends had become the temporary land guardians and were doing quite well with it for a long time. In our fable, one of the owls started teaching an intonement that was slightly off, but he did not realize it until later. So we are going to take what we are learning in this book and apply the same principles to him and his situation.

Now of course, owls are wonderful, intelligent creatures who are very much loved and honored. But how could our owl teacher have caught the error when it happened? As you know, dear readers, he probably should have been more aware and awake, shouldn't he have? He should have been more present and more aware *in that moment*, and then the toning difference might have been corrected immediately — or at least before any more collateral damage had occurred — isn't that true? If he had done that, then the owlet students would have been able to do the toning correctly — more accurately — from the very beginning.

This is not to say that errors can never occur, because we all know that they can sometimes; of course, no one is perfect. And we're sure that our owl friend, the teacher, did not mean to do make this mistake — of course not! But here's our point: If the teacher had been *more aware* in the moment, then he probably would have caught his own error when it occurred, wouldn't he? Of course, we know he would have wanted to. Being more in that moment would have served as a check — as in checks and balances — and would have served as backup for him to double check the accuracy of what he was teaching *before* it was taught, not after.

So you see, we love our owl friend! He's a good owl — very smart, very astute usually. But had he detected and caught his own error immediately, it would have served him, his little owlet fledglings, and Earth much better, wouldn't it?

So there is a prime example in this fable, then, of one of the major principles outlined in this book. You can definitely see how one of the principles plays out in a real situation, can't you? Nobody wants to incur an error, of course, but if you are more in the moment — if you are more aware of it *at the time* — then many, many consequences could be averted or avoided. It would raise the probability quotient for success in any endeavor by quite a bit, wouldn't it?

We are trying to give you all — and our owl friend here — a better chance at success and create an in-house system for the advancement of humankind and owl-kind.

The Earth, the Sun, and Galactic Forces

Now it has been given that the energies of Earth are very affected by what is happening with your Sun. The gravity pull of Earth is affected by, of course, two things: centrifugal force and centripetal force. But did you also know that it is affected by sunspots? And the activity on the Sun is affected by something called solar winds. Solar winds are caused by the movements of galaxies and stars, and indirectly by our own galaxy's movement through the cosmos itself. Einstein's theory of relativity itself has been upgraded to $E=MC^3$ — cubed instead of squared!

What is happening out there affects what happens on this planet, and vice versa. If you were to make a paper mâché ball and pretend it was Earth, then make another one somewhat larger and designate it as the Sun, and whirl the first one around the second one, that would be centrifugal force, wouldn't it? Then, if you were able to rotate that first one as it went around your Sun, that would be centripetal force, would it not? But what if you took the second ball, your Sun, and threw it across a large room while magically keeping the planet circling and rotating, then the force on both the Sun *and* the Earth would be affected, would it not?

So what you have then is a third force acting on the first two already in motion. That third force would be what is happening right now, because our Sun and all in its orbit are moving across our galaxy at a rapid rate of speed. So all these forces not only affect the gravity of the planet, but they also affect the harmonics of the planet. Our planet needs daily adjustments to its harmonics, and what used to only need yearly adjustments now needs daily work to keep everything in balance, both here on Earth and out in the nearby vicinity of our own galaxy.

We wanted to make an additional comment about the fact that many of you are worried that the owls caused problems for Earth; they did not! As with the otter story, there was a reason why these animals were chosen to represent, or make allusion to, something else. Again, as before, we needed an animal to set up the framework for the story — that is all. Owls are good and wonderful creatures, and were only used, as we've said, to be able to talk about Earth and what the whales do for her that is so very valuable to her existence and the continuation of life here on this planet.

Please do not worry that the owls are in trouble or actually caused harm — no! This is a fable, and as such, certain parts were fabricated to reach out to our readers for your concern and understanding of the ins and outs, the intricacies, and purposes for which these tales were created. Whales by their very nature and makeup are extremely intelligent and wonderful creatures of the deep who are just this side of being sentient, and they deserve more respect, love, and understanding for what they do for the oceans and the planet than they usually get.

The great majority of people on this planet simply do not understand what the cetaceans — whales, in particular — are all about. We simply wanted to get the word out to as many as possible to stop, for instance, using them for food for your dinner table. Whales are not food or anything close to it, and anything nutritional they could have provided can be synthesized or easily replaced. We are just trying to wake everybody up! No whale should ever have to fear that it be hunted and killed. For each whale you slaughter, there will then be hundreds, if not more, of what would have been their progeny slaughtered, too. This truly is the "killing of the innocents," and we need people to make some basic amendments to their thoughts, attitudes, and what is on their dinner plates. We love you all so much, but you are killing the planet every time you kill a whale. They are beautiful, beautiful creatures and have already done so much for everyone and everything here. All they want from us is to be appreciated more and used and abused less!

12

The Centurion

There once was a figure of great stature and strength named Koracus. Koracus was a Roman centurion of ancient times. He had grown up in a patrician family. His father was a high-ranking official in the government of that time and place. Koracus was a child with many good traits. He was smart, well built, and agile, with a keen eye and quick reflexes. He had a good head for mathematics and academics, and he excelled in all his classes. But Koracus, for all his good qualities, was a very lazy boy. He was also quite a time waster and would wait until the last minute with almost every task. This drove his family to distraction, and they were constantly having to nag and prod him to get anything done — his studies, his chores (not many, as his family was wealthy, but he still had a few assigned duties), and so forth.

Now you, dear reader, are probably wondering how this Koracus came to be a centurion after such an inauspicious and ignoble start. You see, he met a person along the way who befriended him and inspired him to greatness, who taught him to work hard and to expect more of himself, who inspired him to see the real person deep inside himself: the brave, courageous, and noble person who was already there. So here is our story — and it is a fascinating one.

One day as Koracus was starting a new class, the obligatory soldier training required of every young Roman boy of that time, he met a new classmate named Demetrianos. Demetrianos was not Roman but of Thracian-Grecian heritage. You see, his parents had been captured and sold into slavery when they were very young by an invading army. They met working as slaves in the same household of a high official in Corinth. Over time, they were both so loyal and hardworking that their owner set them free. They had fallen in love while working as household slaves and married soon after they'd been freed. They set up a humble but noble home, making silver and gold trinkets and selling them in the daily marketplace for a modest profit.

They soon had three children: two younger girls and Demetrianos, the oldest. Demetrianos's parents had a strong work ethic from their slavery days, and they taught their children that working hard was something that was highly valued in their family and in their world.

On the other hand, it so happened that Koracus, in the way that young people often do, kept stalling his parents about going to "gladiator school," as he called it — a derogatory term for a boy of his station and time.

"Why do I even have to go?" he whined to his father. "I just know I'm going to hate it, having to get up so early and practice all day every day in the hot sun. Why do I have to do this?"

To which his father gave the wise and timeless reply for restless, lazy teenagers: "Because your mother and I want you to go. Because it will be good for you."

Koracus had no argument for that, and he sullenly agreed to go.

Demetrianos, on the other hand — and on the other side of the city — couldn't wait to go. When he heard that his father had secured a place for him at the school, it was all he could talk about for months. And so both young men showed up for the first day of class. Each of the new trainees was outfitted with all the necessary accouterments for the four-month class: a broadsword, shield, helmet, and the necessary fighting gear, all made from handmade leather with brass studs and fittings. The fighting school also had its own used swords of wood and metal of differing sizes and weights that the students could use, depending on their physical size, weight, and heft. When Koracus received his, he frowned and grimaced, looking down. As Demetrianos took his, his face beamed with enthusiasm, excitement, and anticipation. The two young men glanced at each other, taking each other's measure. Their eyes met and they nodded in acknowledgment of each other. Neither one of them knew what they were in for or that this first meeting would be the beginning of a long relationship that would change the course of both their lives.

Koracus and Demetrianos, having just met for the first time, did not have an immediate liking for each other. In fact, they did not like each other at all at first. Demetrianos thought Koracus was a stuck-up, spoiled, lazy brat who was too used to luxury and easy living. Koracus, on the other hand, thought Demetrianos was just a gung-ho "yahoo" with muscles but no brains or culture.

"Who does he think he is?" Koracus snarled. "He actually thinks this is going to be fun? Boy, is he in for a rude awakening!"

Demetrianos, in turn, had no good things to say about Koracus either. "What a deluded know-it-all! He doesn't know how lucky he is to be in this kind of training school. He's such a complainer! He needs to just shut his mouth and listen. He might actually learn a thing or two, that's for sure!" Demetrianos said to himself, shaking his head in derision.

The next morning at dawn, everyone was woken up rudely by the blaring of a large horn on a parapet at the edge of the arena. The students ran out, formed lines, and stood at attention. "You are now at the Roman Academy of Arms and Weaponry. We will teach you basic and advanced techniques of how to use each one of these weapons. But this school will also take you boys and turn you into fighting men! You will rise every day at dawn and assemble for roll call on the parade grounds. We will teach you everything you will need to know. You will also learn how to take care of your weapons, clean and polish them, and keep them in good order. There will be no shirking of any duties, and all will be treated with the same courtesy and respect. Dis-missed!"

And with that, they all headed out for the mess hall to get something to eat, then scrambled back to their quarters to get ready for the first lesson of the day.

After that, day after day, the students were put through their paces: first, reveille and roll call, then a quick breakfast, then to practice. Demetrianos and Koracus continued to glare at each other every day across the practice field. Both excelled at learning the techniques of soldiering. Then one day toward the end of the training, they were paired with each other in practice. This was not to either one's liking, but they each fought well. Again, they were taking each other's mettle and temperament when they sparred. On this day, however, the lesson master called for the two of them to spar in front of the entire class — a real fighting match!

Both boys by now had become highly skilled in the weaponry and armaments of their day and time. They were still not fond of each other, but this day was very different. This would be a day neither would ever forget! On this day, they were prepared to spar with real weapons — not the wooden ones used in the usual daily practice. This time they were using real swords.

The signal was given, and they began. Lunging and striking, parrying and jabbing, swiftly back and forth they went at each other. Swords clashing and shining in the sun — it was an epic battle! On and on they went. What a match it was! But after a while, they both begin to tire. Demetrianos, for all his great strength and stamina, began to look strained as he raised his sword arm. Swooping the sword down in a lateral motion, he nearly slashed Koracus's left shoulder. Koracus dropped low quickly, the sword barely missing him. He, too, was feeling the heat and the strain, and he had to admit to himself that Demetrianos's strength, skill, and stamina surpassed his own. He was beginning to fear that he might not survive the bout, and he finally realized that his prior slothfulness and lack of stamina and energy might just bring him down at the hands of someone he had previously thought he was superior to. But something in Demetrianos's eyes made him realize that his opponent did not hate him after all.

Suddenly Koracus found himself lying on the ground, Demetrianos's sword poised to strike. But instead of plunging in a death blow, he reached down and took Koracus by the forearm and pulled him up, grinned, and said, "Koracus, my friend, you are a worthy opponent. You almost had me several times. It was an honor to fight you! Let us be at peace with each other, my brother."

Koracus just stood there, stunned and exhausted, but curiously exhilarated. He'd never had to fight so hard in his whole life — but suddenly he felt great! A newfound feeling of self-respect went through him, and he grinned back and said, "Okay, okay. Peace, my brother — peace. Yes, let us bury the sword between us. I know now that we both only wanted the same thing — to win. You, too, are a worthy opponent and a noble man. Come — let us go eat!"

They both grinned again and hugged each other at their newfound friendship. Both of them had won the day!

Demetrianos and Koracus discovered that they could be friends after all, even though there were many, many differences between them. The moral principle in play here, among others, is called conflict resolution. And what we have not told you, dear readers, is "the rest of the story …"

Entitlement, a Skewed Worldview

While they were at the gladiator school, both of them had come far in their personal journeys from their family circumstances growing up. You see, Koracus, the son of privilege and wealth, never really had to push himself that hard growing up. He had small duties that his father would occasionally ask him to do, but for the most part there was nothing, really, for him to strive for or push himself to achieve. And a child who grows up in this manner learns many of the wrong things about himself and about how to treat others, including those in his inner family unit. Children thus brought up have a skewed worldview, one in which they are, or they feel they are, the center of the universe and are therefore entitled to this and that. Thinking of other people and their needs and wants is always a huge afterthought with people like this.

Now, we don't want you to get the wrong impression here about Koracus. He was a good kid, as we described before; it's just that his wealth and privilege weakened him as a person, weakened his character. He didn't ever have to work very hard for anything, and in the training school he had to work hard for everything. Even getting up that early in the morning was a major challenge for him, especially at first. But Koracus got into the rhythm of it, and it became easier. He was then put through his paces by the different teachers of the various methods and disciplines of the school.

He was, at first, very conflicted about being there, and his major battle was not with learning the techniques but within himself. He needed to resolve his inner conflicts and attitudes about who he was. An identity crisis of immense proportions was at play here. Day by day, he plugged away at that too. He realized that because he wanted to excel, he would have to work on himself on the inside too in order to meet the challenges that were always there on the outside. So he did an admirable job, this Koracus, of learning and advancing forward in the school. Another factor was him meeting Demetrianos.

Demetrianos, it seemed to Koracus, already had many of the attributes needed at the school. He was used to hard work and used to getting up early. He was extremely physically fit, especially for his age. Demetrianos had an easy confidence about him that Koracus secretly envied, as Koracus was all bravado on the surface, but underneath felt weak and inadequate in certain tasks. Koracus could be cocky too, but underneath he suffered from low self-esteem. So Demetrianos's seemingly easy confidence and self-assurance was something that Koracus admired but, as of yet, had not been able to achieve for himself.

Character and Integrity: Rising to the Challenge

In those days of ancient Rome, it was a common occurrence for young men to be required to test their mettle against each other at gladiator schools before they reached manhood to help determine what they would best be suited for. Even sons of high-ranking officials and wealthy families were expected to make a showing at these training schools. The parents of such sons as Koracus expected them to go and do their best — and try not to get hurt in the process. Many of the sons of the wealthy went and would just go through the mōtions, not really applying themselves, because they figured they would get an appointment as an officer anyway, no matter how they did. However, our Koracus was not such a young man.

At first, he did the same things as the other rich kids and just kind of laid around and coasted. But one training master saw something in Koracus that the other boys did not have. He thought he saw a spark of something in him — the spirit of a real warrior. So he yelled at him more and gave him extra practices and different things to do to try to shake him loose from his lazy ways, to get him to do something more. He challenged him every day, and Demetrianos was in the background just grinning, watching poor Koracus get pushed to the limit. However, slowly Koracus began to respond. He found out quickly that he liked the very physical hand-to-hand combat they were doing each day, and as "muscle-upon-sinew-upon-character" flexed and strengthened, he started practicing more on his own. He would actually get up early to get in some extra practice before everyone else rose for the day. The practice master secretly applauded his efforts, as they confirmed to him exactly what he had felt about Koracus all along. He had it in him, but he had to be pushed hard to get to it!

Eternal Friends

When it came time to have the showdown between Koracus and Demetrianos, both young men were ready. Koracus was still not in as good of shape as Demetrianos, nor did he have that kind of physical stamina yet, but he held his own. As we said before, the sword fight was a long one, and both young men were beginning to tire. Demetrianos outlasted Koracus but chose not to inflict a real wound; instead, he offered a hand up in respect and new friendship. Koracus had never had a friend like Demetrianos. They became fast friends, and you could see them each day talking, laughing, and horsing around. Each one learned a lot about the other's background, family history, and culture, and this expanded them both. Demetrianos learned more about what it was really like to grow up in a wealthy family — the advantages and disadvantages. Koracus learned from Demetrianos just how hard, yet rewarding, it could be growing up as the son of freed slaves. Koracus learned about Demetrianos's biggest asset: his work ethic. And Koracus started learning that hard work and discipline were not dirty words, and that there were unseen rewards down the road for those who could master both.

Back to the Story …

Koracus and Demetrianos, after they had completed school, joined the Roman army of that day and time, both as junior non-commissioned officers. They both ended up training the new recruits and enjoyed putting them through the boot camp environment they had just come from. And after each group graduated, they would start in on the newcomers.

Demetrianos and Koracus worked well together, and both had become so skilled that occasionally the new recruits would ask them to spar with each other just to see a demonstration of how skilled and how good they could be if they applied themselves as Koracus and Demetrianos had done. Their training school got a reputation for excellence, and instead of avoiding soldier training, they had young men lining up to get in — if only to see Koracus and Demetrianos go at it!

Now, after a few years and many actual battles, Koracus decided to stay in the army. After he was promoted to the rank of centurion, he decided to stay and make it his career. However, after Koracus decided to stay, Demetrianos felt drawn back home. His parents were very aged by then, and he wanted to go be with them because, after all, they had made him what he was.

So Koracus and Demetrianos parted ways. Demetrianos never made it back, however. Years later Koracus heard a rumor that he had died unfortunately in a freak accident. Demetrianos happened to be on his way somewhere and was standing by the side of a road when suddenly a cascade of boulders fell on him, crushing him. Koracus mourned deeply when he heard the news, and he silently thanked his old friend for what he had given him: a life of strength, courage, respect, and honor.

Demetrianos and Koracus became best friends, and both of them became men. There's a little more to the story than meets the eye, though. You see, dear readers, Koracus was the only son of a senator, who was expected to follow in his father's footsteps and become a politician of those times. However, Koracus found out that he liked being a soldier and wanted to stay in the army. His father disapproved. After all, the sons of senators usually became tribunes without having to do much to earn the title. Most soldiers in the Roman army snickered and resented these rich boys playing at being officers. Not only did they usually not deserve the title, but they were never really respected by the men under them, either.

Koracus knew this. During the years that he and Demetrianos were in training school, he found out that his father had arranged for him to be granted the rank of tribune because he was the son of a senator. His father had gotten the job for him. But he did not want it — if he was going to rise in rank, he thought, it was going to be through his own effort and hard work, not because his father had gotten him the job. Also, and much more important to him personally, he had worked hard to earn the respect of the men under him. Respect meant much more to him than rank. So he turned his father down. His father was deeply offended and all but ostracized him from the family. He let Koracus know that he was no longer welcome in his house. Koracus in turn was quite hurt and angry that his father didn't respect or understand how hard he had worked, how much he had changed for the better.

So from then on, when our two soldiers had time off, Koracus would go to stay with Demetrianos's family, who had resettled in Greece. He got to know Demetrianos's mother, father, and sisters very well, and he became very fond of them. After many years, when Demetrianos had gone home for good to be with his sisters just before their parents died, Koracus considered going with him, but he stayed behind because he had grown to love his career. During the years following, he met a lovely lady. They were secretly married and had three children, two girls and a boy. Koracus would be gone for months at a time, but his wife loved him very much and waited patiently. She knew that he was the happiest when he was out working.

Eventually, Koracus and his parents reconciled. His dad, now very elderly, had mellowed and finally accepted Koracus's decision to stay with his men in a position he grew to love. His mother had missed him terribly over the years, and she wept the first time her son walked into his old family home after so many years. Koracus's wife and children accompanied him on that first visit back, and he introduced them to his parents for the first time. Koracus's parents accepted his wife as part of their family and invited her and the children to come and live with them. She accepted.

Koracus lived a long and happy life, but he missed his good friend Demetrianos sorely for the rest of his days. He had a small stone dedicated to him erected in the center of the family garden. The stone read:

To My Friend Demetrianos
May you Rest in Peace
You deserve a place in Heaven
And may you now become the Spiritual Warrior
And fight for Kingdoms unknown
And sail on crystal waters
For saving me from myself
Goodbye My Best Friend, Goodbye

Koracus died eventually too, and his wife and family put up another stone right beside the one for Demetrianos. All it said was:

To Koracus, who rests beside
Demetrianos
Whose Friendship withstood the test of Time
May you Rest in Peace
Beloved Husband, Father, Friend
and true Spiritual Warrior

The Fighting Bout: A Different Perspective

We have our two men who were best friends and so integral in each other's lives. You read the touching tribute to Demetrianos that Koracus put on a stone and placed in an honored part of his family garden. When Koracus passed, his wife placed him beside his friend's commemorative stone because that's where she knew he would have wanted to be.

We are returning to a certain portion of the story because we want to give you a bit of an overview from a different perspective. We want you to imagine that you are there in the middle of the fighting bout and that you can read Demetrianos's mind as he is fighting Koracus. So here we go:

Well, this should be interesting. I should be able to defeat him easily. I've seen him get up early and go out to the practice field, but — who does he think he is? Does he think he can beat me? Hmm … we shall soon see who is whose master! The bout begins. Ugh … he's a little better than I thought he was … ugh … he got a good one in there! I didn't expect that. I didn't realize he had this kind of skill. I really didn't. I thought it would be easy to defeat him, but this … is … not what I expected at all! He almost got me in the arm, but I threw myself back in time. Ah! I'm starting to get really tired. And it hurts when I raise my sword arm. Whoa, man, he is good — he's really good. Hey — maybe he's not my equal, but he's pretty close. Whew! Getting real tired now. Sure wish this would be over, but I'm not going down. You know, he's a lot like me actually, deep down. I've got more stamina, though. But he's got a lot of fight in him — a lot of heart! Okay, here it is. He got tired and made a mistake. I've got him … I've got him. But I can't do it now — I can't finish him. He's okay. He's become a man after all!

From Dislike to Respect: Opening to Change

We wanted to let you see how Demetrianos went from disliking Koracus to respecting him, and what his process was. That bout was a turning point for both young men. Koracus learned what hard work and discipline can bring, and Demetrianos was able to see beyond the "spoiled rich kid" persona that Koracus came in with. Demetrianos was willing to open his mind to change.

The two men had a destiny with each other, did they not? And, as you have observed, each one had a strength that the other did not. Koracus had the advantage of wealth and position but was severely lacking in strength of character; Demetrianos, on the other hand, did not grow up with the advantages of privilege, but he more than made up for it in hard work, determination, discipline, and attitude.

Each one had what the other lacked, but when they met, there was no instant recognition, acknowledgement, or awareness of this at all. In fact, they disliked each other at first. So let's look at that, shall we? What causes certain people to like each other, and what causes other people to dislike each other (other than basic karmic overlay from previous incarnations together)? Let's see if we can analyze this a little more closely.

When two people first meet, what you must understand is that an extremely complex energy assessment goes on between them. There are different personality energy types, as outlined so well in Dr. Barbara Brennan's book *Hands of Light*. In a sense, different personality types react differently with each other. The energies "sniff each other out" in the actual meeting and assessment stage, and then they either accept the energy, rebuff it, or block it. When there is a rebuff, you can tell if one person is not accepting of another's energy field by his or her body language. For example, the person doing the blocking will stand back a bit, perhaps with the arms folded across the chest — this is the classic rebuff stance.

When Koracus and Demetrianos first met, they rebuffed each other right off the bat. That was the beginning of their relationship. They did not feel or recognize the energies of a previous incarnation yet, although they could have if they'd been more in touch with subtle energies. Their first impressions of each other were negative, but first impressions are not always the best indicator of what the quality of that relationship might be later on.

Secondly, each relationship, as psychologists well know, has a certain dynamic to it — a quality, a feel about it — that can change over time.

This can change because of the free will of each individual to decide to take away the blocks or not, and much of this is according to the other's moods, emotionality, attitude, and previous life associations, to name a few. So you see, this can be quite a complex function.

The Energetic Handshake

There is a lot that goes on when people first meet. So if, like our two young men, they don't like each other at first but are open-minded, amenable, and ready to evolve, then transformation of negative energy into positive energy can occur. Each young man, over the course of his training, kept testing the waters each day when he encountered the other. It was a bit like a challenge between two types of energy fields that are always in flux according to many factors (but mainly mood, temperament, and personality). So in a way, when they first met, they both sensed that there was something more between them — a previous life together. And there was, in addition to everything else, a deep and intense energetic recognition of that. But both young men misinterpreted that feeling as dislike, when it was really just a huge energetic recognition and handshake! It wasn't *real* dislike — it was an acknowledgment of the other person that each felt so deeply, but in their young minds they interpreted it as dislike. All it really was was an energetic handshake!

13

The Tentmaker

Once there was a man named Joseph. Joseph lived in olden times, so this is not a modern-day story. He was the son of a tentmaker, who in those days was quite wealthy. The making of a good tent takes considerable skill and finesse, along with knowledge of mathematics, engineering, and artistry. All those skills and more are necessary ingredients for what will become a beautiful and elaborate tent with intricate and lovely weavings, fine silks, and other fabrics that can be used. The finished product can be a beautiful work of art fit for a sultan.

Our fellow Joseph was trained in the fine art of tentmaking, and in that day and time it was considered a highly respected profession to be in because it was both honorable and lucrative. He learned from his father and uncle well and continued on in the family business, but he also wanted to be something else. He wanted to become a carpenter, as he loved working with wood. As a young boy, he had another uncle, a master craftsman who, with his strong sons, built houses in the town where they lived.

Joseph used to love to go visit this other uncle, Halleliel, when he was working on a house. He would get permission from his mother, and then he would run across the little town to the job site where were working to just stand around and watch the workmen. The smell of the freshly cut wood, the hammering of the nails, watching how the joints would fit together — he found it familiar and, in a way, comforting. His uncle would sometimes let him hammer or hold something — he was still quite young — while it was being sawed, and he just loved it. Then later he would hurry back to get home by dinnertime.

His mother would remind him that soon he would be spending all of his time learning to make tents with his father, Joseph Sr., and other uncle, Ken. He would always tell his mother that he wanted to be a woodmaker instead.

"No, Joseph," his mother would say. "You must honor your father's wishes and become a tentmaker like him. It is a very respected and honorable profession, and one in which we know our family tradition will go on. Your other uncle, Halleliel, just works with wood because he was no good at tentmaking, so he found something else to do. There is not much else you can do in this town, Joseph. You may go and visit him, but not too often. There are things for you to do here, too, around our house. And your studies, Joseph — don't neglect your studies."

"Okay, Mother. I won't," was all Joseph would say. Then he would go off by himself to his room.

"Yes, I know I have to concentrate on my studies and read my books," he thought to himself. "But I really like working with wood. I like being around it and everything about it, but my parents think I should concentrate on tents. I have been learning how to do it. Father has begun to train me. I like it all right — I can do it. I can learn how to do it and do it well, but …"

It would always be the same conversation between Joseph and his mother — every time. She would remind him about his duty to the family business, and he would listen patiently and try to explain his love of wood, but each time it was to no avail. Then he would quietly go to his room, lay on his bed, and think, as young men often do.

As the years went by, Joseph found himself engrossed in the tentmaking business with his father and uncle. He had learned the trade very well and had become a businessman, too — like them. He had gone into business with them, in fact, and he had no time to even visit his other uncle anymore. How he missed the sights and the smells! Even the loud sounds of the hammering were like music to his ears. But he was stuck.

Joseph never forgot about his love and desire for working with wood. It would probably be another ten or so years before he was able to leave the tentmaking profession to try to learn carpentry and woodwork; however, his Uncle Halleliel was still alive, so Joseph was sometimes able to sneak away on an errand and be there for two or three hours on an off day. His father and uncle in the tentmaking business had never wanted him to even try to learn it, because they thought that "a man should only concentrate on one thing at a time in order to be the best tentmaker there is." That was what they were always telling him.

"If you say so," Joseph would say, thinking otherwise. Then he would also think to himself that someday he was going to stop making tents and do what *he* really wanted to do!

So Joseph kept sneaking away to work with Uncle Halleliel, and he was learning how to do things very rapidly. His learning curve accelerated when Halleliel told him how good he was getting and that he really had a knack for it. He just felt as if this was where he belonged, but he was afraid to tell his father that he no longer wanted to be a tentmaker.

But one fatal day it happened, and he was found out. His uncle just happened to be on a real errand and was walking by the job site where Joseph was working when he saw him. He stayed hidden but rushed across town to tell Joseph's father what he had seen.

Joseph's father was extremely angry and hurt, for he had wanted to hand down the business to Joseph, and now he felt betrayed. When Joseph arrived back from his supposed errand, his father was livid. They started yelling back and forth. Joseph did not want to argue with or hurt his father, but he just could not get him to listen. So he felt he had no choice but to quietly quit. After his father said something terrible about him, he turned and walked away. His father came running after him, accusing him of disrespect and ingratitude.

Joseph told him quietly that he had meant no disrespect, nor was he ungrateful, but that he had tried many times to speak with his father about this. His father would always cut him off and make fun of it. And — as a last effort — Joseph pleaded with his father to understand that he had given over ten years of loyal service to something that he truly did not like.

He had stuck with it because he knew it was what his father wanted. He then asked his father if he cared about him at all.

His father said, yes, he did, but — Joseph interrupted, saying that if he truly cared about his son, he would have wanted him to be happy. His father stopped for a moment and thought about that. In that moment he realized that Joseph was right — he *did* want Joseph to be happy, but he had wanted him to be happy doing what he wanted him to do, not what Joseph really wanted.

And so, Joseph reminded him that he had wanted to work with wood since he was a little boy. His father, finally realizing that he had caused the situation, turned and said to him, "Then, my boy, you go and be a carpenter, if that is truly what makes you happy."

"It is, Father. It is."

So they were able to speak their truth to each other after all those years had gone by — finally.

14

The Gift

Once upon a time, there was a man named Bartholomew. Bartholomew knew that he was not going to live much longer, so he prepared himself, in various ways, to die. Now, this man Bartholomew had a friend named Ishmael. Although Bartholomew and Ishmael were from very different families and traditions, they loved each other very much and were as brothers. For you see, Ishmael had saved Bartholomew's life when they were young. They had grown up in the same village and played together as boys. They were childhood friends and had many adventures together, as young boys will do.

One day, as they were playing, a deadly snake approached — a cobra! Bartholomew started backing away, although his family and neighbors had told him not to move if one was seen. But being a young boy, he panicked and took a few steps backward, falling into a small but deep ravine. Ishmael, however, did not panic, and as he watched his friend fall back into the ravine, the thought came to him of what to do. He grabbed a nearby stick and, showing great courage, threw it sideways at the great snake, hitting it broadside and almost knocking it over. The snake, thus surprised, slithered away back from where it had come.

Ishmael ran up to the edge of the ravine, almost crying at the thought that his good friend could be lying dead or mortally wounded at the bottom of it. As he knelt carefully down to look over the edge, he saw his friend hanging on to a large root from one of the trees common to the area — a large cedar tree of many, many years. The root was thick and very strong. Bartholomew had been able to grab hold of it at the last second as he was falling!

Now this Ishmael, who was a very smart young man, quickly sized up the dire situation that his friend was in and yelled to the other boys to come quickly. He told them to form a line behind him, as he knew he would have to lie down over the edge and hang far over to reach his friend. And he did so. As the other boys held Ishmael, he reached way down and grabbed Bartholomew, then yelled for everybody to pull. They gave a mighty heave, and instantly Bartholomew was pulled from impending danger.

The boys became even closer after this and maintained their friendship throughout many years and many circumstances of life, family, and friends. Through good times and bad, even war and strife, the strength of their love and friendship withstood the test of years.

Now, as we know from the beginning of the story, Bartholomew had been stricken with a sudden but serious illness, and he prepared himself for the inevitable. His wife had already passed over, and his grown-up children all lived far away. His friend Ishmael now lived in a neighboring village, and they would occasionally visit each other. When Ishmael heard about Bartholomew's condition, he rushed over. And when Ishmael saw Bartholomew, he immediately knew that his dear friend was ready to pass on.

Tenderly they embraced each other for the last time, and Bartholomew said, "You know, Ishmael, I never quite properly thanked you for saving my life all those years ago. We were so young back then and ended up laughing it off as young boys do. But I want to give you something that I have saved over these many years. I always intended to give it to you, but I could never quite find the right moment. But here it is. It is a piece of my heart — a beautiful stone that I grabbed at the last moment when I was being pulled up from hanging on to that cedar root. As I was holding on for dear life, I saw something glinting in the sun and reached for it as you and our friends were pulling me up. I had quickly put it in my pocket at the time, but later when I was alone, I took it out to look at it and, lo — it was a beautiful diamond stone encrusted with gold and with a golden clasp that must have fallen from a necklace and gotten buried deep in the sand. I never told anyone about it, not even my wife, for I knew that it was a gift from God and was meant to go to the one man who had saved my life — you! So here it is. May God in his infinite mercy always bless you, my dear friend."

And Bartholomew lay back onto his pillows and died. Ishmael, full of tears but also full of heart, took the magnificent jewel and put it in a secret place, for they had been alone in the room at the time.

By and by, Ishmael had the stone appraised and was told that the jewel had fallen from the necklace of a great emir's wife from a caravan that had gone by their village almost a hundred years before — and was worth the equivalent of a million dollars! The great-great-grandson of the emir, hearing about the great stone, came and paid that amount to the astounded Ishmael, who handed over the great jewel. With all that money, Ishmael was able to help his village, Bartholomew's village, and the whole surrounding area of their country that had been devastated by a war over twenty years before.

And for the rest of his life, Ishmael went around doing many good things with the money. Each time a building was repaired, a street rebuilt, or someone's livelihood restored, his heart was warmed by the tremendous gift that had been bequeathed to him from his dear friend, Bartholomew. And he knew that it was a precious gift of love for all!

15

Julio and Marcus

Once there was a forest trail guide named Julio. Julio was a very good man who loved to ride horses. He not only loved to ride them, but he loved the horses that he rode and took very good care of them. In his job as a trail guide, he oftentimes would stop his trail group as they were walking along to gaze at and gather the flora along the way, to take some samples, for the forest was a place where he felt at home and at peace.

You see, Julio had grown up alongside a great, very old river that occasionally had large ponds along its long route to the sea. And the very small town that he grew up in was famous in the area for the sugar beets that grew so well there. Although the forest around the town was essentially a rainforest, Julio and his brothers learned to love all the different kinds of forests, and each one of the seven of them grew up studying different kinds of forests. But Julio loved them all and became an expert in each.

Julio's love for the forests of his world was surpassed by his love for animals, particularly horses. His father did not have a ranch, but they raised plenty of horses, as they were the main mode of transportation in that day and time. Julio's favorite one was a steed they named Marcos — Marcos the Magnificent. He was a great, beautiful chestnut-colored horse with a fine mane and tail. Julio and Marcos formed a very close bond. They both loved each other and were very devoted to one another. Each one could almost read the mind and heart of the other, and when they went riding about, they were as one mind, one heart — almost one soul. Everyone who saw them knew this to be true, and they became well known in the local area.

As Julio grew up, he realized that someday he would be leaving his small town and going out into the world, for he sensed that there was something outside, some great mission that needed to be accomplished. So when he reached a certain point of maturity and manhood, he and his beloved horse Marcos left for a foreign land far away. Julio went by boat so that he and Marcos could travel together. Many, many miles stood between Julio's country and what would soon be his new home, and the trip was very, very long and arduous, but Julio and Marcos stayed together and rode out each storm and each setback with relative ease and grace. They made it to the far shore — they had found a new home!

When they arrived on the shore of what would eventually become home for them, Julio knew no one. He did not yet even know how to speak the language, but he felt strongly in his heart that this new place was where his future destiny lay. Intelligent, unafraid, and hardworking, he was quick to learn new things. Knowing that he needed to find a place for himself and his horse, he quickly procured a job at a local stable near the coastal city where he had landed.

Julio worked there happily for a while, learning the new language, taking care of the horses and Marcos, and making new friends. When people from all over came there to board their horses, they immediately noticed Julio riding around on Marcos. Marcos stood out, since he was such a beautiful and strong horse who held his head high. They made quite an impression on everyone and there were many offers to buy Marcos, but Julio always refused to sell him, as they were still so close. Julio liked it there, but he longed to find a job in which he could use his keen knowledge of forestry and still be able to spend as much time with Marcos as he could.

After a time, a certain couple came to the stables with an inquiry. They had just become trustees of a very large parcel of land in the interior. After making inquiries, they wondered if Julio would come and watch over the land for them, as they were very wealthy and traveled a lot. Julio, they thought, could bring Marcos along with him and ride all around and watch things for them during the times that they were gone, which were frequent. So, Julio saw this opportunity — and he took it.

They brought him and Marcos to their ranch beside a very large, beautiful forest — a perfect place! And Julio and Marcos were able to be together every day, riding all over the new, unsullied territory. He knew that it was the perfect place for him and Marcos the Magnificent.

One day when Julio was out riding, they happened upon a snake in the path. Marcos spooked as horses do, and he threw Julio back against a large tree limb, slashing an artery in his arm. Julio lay on the ground, dazed but basically unhurt — except for the gash on his arm. He knew that he had to stop the bleeding fast, so he put a tourniquet around his arm above the wound. But it still wouldn't stop bleeding.

Julio knew he had to get back up on Marcos and get back to the main house, miles away. Thinking quickly, he looked around, and with his knowledge of the plant life of the forest, he found a shrub that he knew would staunch the bleeding. He ran over to the bush, grabbed a bunch of it and held it tightly to the gash. The bleeding slowed down, then mostly stopped as he pressed on it. Then he spat on the wad of herbs in his hand, made a poultice of it, and put it quickly back on, retying the tourniquet over it to keep pressure on the wound and keep the poultice in place. With that he jumped up on Marcos and sped toward the main house. It was still quite a long ride back and there was still some bleeding, but Julio made it there without passing out. A doctor was quickly called and arrived over an hour later. He washed and stitched Julio's wound shut.

Julio recovered, and the rumor went out that he had saved his own life because of his extensive knowledge of forest herbs. People started coming to him from all over to seek out his help for various things, and he became a doctor of sorts in the local area, helping out with everything from childbirth to diseases. Julio became much sought after and had finally found a way he could be of service to humanity. He still had time to take long rides with Marcos in his beloved forest, and he was content. He was able to serve humankind and be the man he had always wanted to be. He was finally home!

* * *

Julio's Dream

As you remember, dear readers, Julio had come from a faraway country to journey to a new world. He left one home and found another. In his newly adopted home, he was able to make new friends, find work in an honorable profession, and make a place for himself and his beloved horse, Marcos, in the new society and in his heart, mind, and soul.

Why did Julio leave his old home in the first place? It was because he felt something stir within him, and in his heart he knew that he needed and wanted to go somewhere else to gift that part of the world with his talents and abilities. Far from leaving because he felt restricted or unfulfilled, he left for the very opposite reason. The place where he grew up was one of the most beautiful areas of the whole Earth. He wanted to take the gifts that his homeland had given him and give them to the world, so he endured an arduous, unpleasant voyage just to find a new garden, if you will, in which to plant himself — and everything he had to give. And what he ended up doing was gifting *himself* — his talents, his expertise, his love, and his soul — the soul of Julio!

Julio had had a good and fulfilling life, and he was one of those people who found his calling and dedication early in life. So we wanted to show in his story how someone like him came to be so dedicated and so aware of his life goal.

As you probably know by now, we all have had previous lives that set up the next ones and so on. Julio's life just previous to this was one in which he had been sickly as a child but grew up to be a doctor, and he was able to be of great service to humanity in that lifetime. So when he came back this time, he did not need to be a doctor again, but he still had the desire to help and to heal.

In a lifetime previous to the one as a doctor, Julio had been an Arab sheik who owned and loved many fine horses for a long time. In that lifetime, his horses were like his children, his family, and he carried that love over across several lifetimes. So are you starting to see, dear readers, that one life can be the culmination or amalgamation of those lives that came before? The things Julio went through, the struggles that he had, the triumphs — all had been brought to bear within his lifetime as Julio.

Many Lifetimes

People reincarnate from lifetime to lifetime to try to improve themselves and their souls, to try to repair and work with their innate weaknesses, and to reap the rewards that they have earned from other lifetimes, because both are brought in each time. Don't you see, dear readers? This can never be done in one lifetime. It just wouldn't make sense, now would it? Achieving perfection in one short lifetime just cannot be done, and it doesn't work that way at all. Your many lives make up who you are today, and your lifetime now will go into the "composite drawing," if you will, for your next one. It is as simple as that!

Of course, what we have given here is a huge oversimplification of a complex but beautiful and inherently logical process for all of us. What god would force us to live only one life and expect absolute perfection? It just isn't so! We all need and go through many, many lifetimes to work with ourselves, improving and refining ourselves each time. Sometimes people get caught up in lifetimes in which they fall back and really mess up, and that is called backsliding. It is unfortunate when this happens, because the forward progress that the soul was making gets halted — or can even occasionally go backward, if a person does a lot of bad or evil things. Again, it is very complex and is individualized for each person.

The Akashic Records

There is an automatic filter that keeps track of everyone's progress — the *akashic records*. Everybody has one of these records, and an absolutely perfect accounting of everything is recorded here. Your thoughts, your emotions — every iota is written on that record, and we just wanted everyone to be aware of it. The Godhead placed it there for everyone, and that's one of the ways each person's life is assessed at its end. So when the future Julio was in between lifetimes, the Spiritual Hierarchy — and many other helpers too — helped him to look at his life just previous to this one and decide what life challenges he wanted and felt he could handle for the next go-around. That way, if he had wanted to choose a different kind of life experience, then he could have done so at that time.

Are you starting to see, dear readers, how this process works? It is a very fine one, and it is not there to punish but to give you guidance on where you are soul-wise and what your options are for rounding yourselves out. Hopefully, you will all avoid certain pitfalls and embrace those things that will help you personally, and even collectively, to progress on the way to the perfection of love in the soul that must happen before you can ascend.

Julio chose to put himself in a situation — his life as Julio — in which he could refamiliarize himself with healing herbs and also have a horse while traveling to a new land that might need his talents and expertise. He ended up far from his birthplace, but he went to a place he had chosen before he incarnated. He did not remember choosing it, but deep in his heart, his soul remembered it and drove him forward to find a place where he could live out his life in service to humanity and still have a beloved life companion — his horse, Marcos!

16

The Shepherd

There was, upon a certain land, a shepherd tending his flock. The night was cold, and as he was watching the sheep, he fell asleep. Then a lioness came in and snatched one of the sheep away and proceeded to kill and eat it. When the shepherd woke up, he saw what had happened, and his natural merriment was taken away and replaced with fear, regret, and a tremendous amount of guilt, as you can imagine.

At this point, he proceeded to pray, saying, "Lord, take this guilt away, for after all, it was dark and I was sleeping. I was supposed to be keeping an eye out for lions, but — oh well, it just couldn't be helped."

However, to himself he secretly said, "If I lie to myself and tell myself it just couldn't be helped, I can then cover up my guilt and pretend it didn't happen, and just put it out of my mind and forget it. I don't really care."

And away he went about his merry way, pretending that he had no real responsibility for the sheep that had lost its life due to his negligence. That really didn't matter to him.

"After all, it was only one sheep," he told himself, continuing on his merry way. It wasn't anything worth having a bad day over. "After all, bad stuff happens," he said to himself.

Night after night, the shepherd would fall asleep, and the lioness would come in and take one sheep. Incredibly, each time the shepherd would tell himself that he had no real responsibility to the flock. Again and again, he would say to himself, "After all, bad things happen." Soon he had said it to himself so many times that his heart had hardened and he no longer cared about the sheep at all. And again, incredibly, he slept soundly each night, oblivious to the lioness and to what was going on, until he no longer cared at all for the sheep.

As his flock dwindled down to the point where there were only a few sheep left, he still — incredibly! — continued to tell himself that everything was all right. But this one night was different. This time the lioness brought her mate and her pride with her, and — you guessed it — they took them all, including the shepherd!

As you can glean from this parable, there were many errors made by the shepherd. Which one do you think was the most glaring error that in the end consumed *him* too? Of course it was the fact that he had become so good at rationalizing what was happening around him that he no longer cared.

He had become so inured to the sheep's suffering, fear, pain, and death, that he no longer even reacted or cared about them at all. In the end, his callousness brought him the same fate as his fellow sheep-brothers.

Sin and Sinning

We are going to explain the differences between sin and sinning. What do these words actually mean? When you say that you have *sinned*, have you simply erred, or was there something deeper going on? Do you simply say your prayers at night and blithely say, "I'm sorry," as if by rote — a shallow and superficial thing that can be easily done, and then just as easily forgiven and forgotten in the blink of an eye?

The shepherd, as we have seen, was rather blithe when he so easily dismissed the first night's killing of the one sheep: "Oh well, bad stuff happens. It doesn't really concern me personally. Why should I bother getting upset by this?" His casual and cavalier attitude about the whole thing did not go any deeper than he allowed it to.

We all know by the telling of the story that he should have cared about the life of his sheep brothers much more than he did. He should have taken it more seriously, cared more deeply, and then perhaps he may have saved his own life in return.

Let us also take a deeper look and see if after the first incident he could or should have thought more deeply by going into his heart and saying, "This is really sad! It was my responsibility for looking after the sheep, and now one's dead because I didn't have enough forethought, or didn't take enough precautions to protect him, and he got eaten! How would *I* have felt in the same sheep-brother situation? I had better move the sheep away to a different area or go find more dogs that bark louder. Maybe I need an assistant here at night so we can take shifts sleeping and each take a watch to ensure future protection of the flock." These are some options that he could have taken, had he cared to. But he just didn't.

So, did he sin? Of course he did — by negligence. But what was the greater sin, then: the first night, or all of the succeeding nights? Which error was greater? The second one, of course! Not because he didn't take the proper precautions, per se, but because he didn't let it sink in deeply enough into his heart — especially after what happened on the first night when he had a chance to do the right thing and effect the changes needed. So the second error was, by far, the worse of the two.When you hear these stories, remember that given within the pages are layers and layers of multiple hidden messages with multiple meanings. The one we gave you had many of these, did it not? We know of the layering and put it there for a purpose.

Lessons and Morals

So what lessons can we learn from this story? There are many. First we learned the obvious ones of selfishness, laziness, and excuse-building. This might be typical of our shepherd, or perhaps he thought he was justified in his continual excuses day after day. Or maybe, just maybe, there were undertones of hate or even malice toward the sheep (or maybe not). Maybe it was the sheer drudgery and tedium of watching sheep day after day that led to resentment of his mundane job setting in, so when the lioness watched and waited, she knew just what night to strike. Perhaps the tediousness that led to boredom and resentment was just enough to open that window of opportunity for the ever-watchful eye of the lioness. Perhaps subconsciously the shepherd was a half-hearted, willing participant in this drama.

When a situation such as the one illustrated arises, there is indeed a moral dilemma, is there not? *Am I my sheep-brother's keeper, or am I not? And what are my inherent moral precepts to be?* Should these decisions be on a purely instinctive level, or made consciously and deliberately determined beforehand? When you are discussing something important like moral issues, you encompass many things. We are here today to make the point that, up until recent history, your Earth has been in the modes of "every man for himself," "dog eat dog," "all spoils go to the strong," and "survival of the fittest." These ideas are not credos so much as the moral dictates of the planet — the unspoken, tacit rules that nobody ever talks about on the surface but everybody adheres to.

We know that humanity, from your earliest known history, believed that it simply went from cavemen to Sumeria and so forth — out of the mud right into recorded history, the history that your scientists have strongly intimated that you have had. We know a different history of Earth, how civilizations truly evolved on this planet, but for now we will go with what is considered a foregone conclusion by most. If you have a circumstance of moral integrity in this day and age, there are varying ways in which this can be acceptably interpreted. Some say it is okay to look to yourself only and do only what is right for yourself. Others say you should take the moral high ground, that *that* is the best way. Still others say that somewhere in the middle should be okay. After all, nobody would blame anyone for that — and so on. You get the picture.

What we are saying is this: There should be a moral code that everyone feels across the board, at the level of the implicit and deeply accepted theories of the heretofore prominent "survival of the fittest" mode, but now focusing on the more enlightened "familial integrity" mode. We are saying that this code should take precedence and should be deeply ingrained into every man, woman, and child on the planet — so deeply that one would only think and act according to that deeply imbedded code of existence: that *all are one*. You are them, and they you.

When this is so upon this planet — a complete 180-degree turnaround from what is acceptable now — then your "new" planet will have advanced considerably, and may yet count itself among the great planets of the stars of this galaxy!

Life's Intrinsic Interconnectedness

The shepherd was totally flummoxed about what to do when one of his sheep was caught in the jaws of a lioness while he frittered away the night sleeping. We know that sleeping at night is what people do — but not when they're supposed to be watching their sheep brothers! We will not belabor the story any further, but the fine point that we are trying to make here with our story is this: We *are* our sheep-brothers' keeper. Because in the end, and also in the beginning, there is only one of you — you are both the shepherd *and* the sheep! Your law of "do unto others as you would have them do unto you" is in operation here in the story just as it is in real life.

The sheep need and are intrinsically connected to the shepherd, and the shepherd is connected to them also. He would have benefitted a lot more had he simply and truly cared about them and seen that doing so was more than a job — it was the business of life itself, life's interconnectedness. Had the shepherd considered that for even five minutes, maybe the first incident would never have happened. Maybe he would have seen the lioness and taken the proper steps to protect the sheep and himself from the very beginning.

Such are the moral dilemmas of real life, and you can now plainly see how truly caring for your "brother" as yourself can have far-reaching consequences for the good. If he had been as one with his brother, the shepherd's caring would have saved his own life too!

Reforming the Shepherd

The shepherd, as you recall, had a moral dilemma on his hands, did he not? And what then did he do? How did he approach his job in his mind and in his heart? First, he disengaged his heart in order to later on make it acceptable, at least in his own mind, to do — or *not* do — the things that he did. His decision-making process was, at that point, disconnected from his heart. As he had made a habit of this, it was pretty easy to do as he always did — a "that makes it okay" kind of thing.

So as he approached this task, his attitude from the outset was pretty *laissez faire*, was it not? "After all," he said to himself, "they're just sheep. No big deal. I can do this — no problem." And then, as you know from the rest of the ill-fated story, one un-heart-connected error after another took place, leading to the demise of all of the sheep and the shepherd as well. So let's look at him and reform him. Let's pretend that we can be with him at the onset of the task and help him in his decision-making process, shall we?

His job is to watch over the sheep. At this moment, let's go into his head and say, as if we were him: "I have this opportunity to take care of and watch over some sheep. Hmm … okay, let's think this through for a few minutes. I need this job, but this job entails watching over this flock of sheep, and I'm beginning to realize that they are not just dumb animals — not quite pets, but possibly they have names and families and … do sheep have emotions? What if they do? Okay then, well, *I* have a family, and *I* have emotions, so … then … oh! What if they are *not* just dumb animals after all? Then they could be more like me than I originally figured. Oh, I see. What if they are *my family*? What if they are like my brothers and sisters? I'm not sure that they are, but then again, I'm not sure that they aren't either. Hmm … wait a minute! I think they *are* my family after all. And after all, I love my family and would never let any harm come to them, so, let's see … and there are quite a lot of them, aren't there? Maybe I should get one of my other shepherd friends to help watch them at night too. Hmm … you know, that might be a really good idea!"

You see, as we were in his head, we helped him at the job's very inception to think about the situation in a very different way — a more heart-centered way. And then once he engaged his heart, he realized that the sheep *were* his brothers after all.

Why do you think, then, that he had the dilemma? And was it a dilemma that you all face from time to time, sometimes every day? What do you do? How should you think about something like this? What should be your mental attitude? What should be your heart attitude? Oftentimes, all these decisions are made very quickly — in a matter of a few minutes. For some, only a few seconds!

Choices and Realities

Let us reflect on the morality issue here. If the shepherd chooses from his old or usual attitude — mainly mental — he will most likely make a moral misstep and choose out of expediency, haste, negligence, or laziness to do whatever is his momentary whim. He apparently does not see the moment for what it really is: an opportunity to be a catalyst for change, to be truly in the moment — aware and awake morally, spiritually, and emotionally. He chooses to do what he usually does and misses the opportunity of that beautiful moment entirely. What does he really see? What does he truly feel for the sheep? Could it be that he is subconsciously afraid to feel anything at all, bidding his heart to be silent and not bother him with pesky and bothersome emotions? Could it be that he feels straitjacketed in some way by constricting and conflicting emotions or moral precepts? And if he cannot resolve this sudden cataclysm of impossible conflicts within himself, would he then make a "nondecision" and forfeit the opportunity to connect his head and heart, making a snap decision based on nothing? He chooses to run away, as usual, from moments like these. So yes, he would choose to not choose, meaning he could defer the decision to a later time — or not choose at all.

We would see then, at that point, that the sheep fade quickly from their chance to be thought of as real and are then "relegated to the woodpile" in the shepherd's mind. They are discarded and put aside, losing both the moment and, ultimately, their lives.

The Shepherd: Just an Ordinary Guy

When the shepherd is first engaged to watch the sheep, he goes through a brief series of assessments of what this particular job entails. During this assessment, he thinks it will be easy. He thinks he knows what to do, but as we know by now, he fatally neglects to correctly assess the seriousness of the job and his real responsibility to it by way of deducing the situation from a purely mental standpoint. There are definite gaps in his learning curve, and he leaves out a few steps here and there. Of course, as we observe him, *we* realize the main error — but he does not see it. His attitude is that the sheep are "just a bunch of dumb animals," which is his overriding thought process throughout the whole situation, and in that moment that just escapes him.

Now, we want you, the reader, to realize some things about the shepherd. He's not a bad guy. He's a regular sort of person from a good, respectable family, is an upstanding citizen of his country, and attends religious services faithfully. He is also intelligent, and he has many friends. He is a devoted husband with a wife and child. The picture we want to paint for you is one of an ordinary man — he's just a regular guy. He is not a bad person in any way; he is a typical man for his country and time.

So let's be clear about the job situation to which he has been assigned. He was hired to watch the sheep because the man who used to be in charge of them was called away on another matter and was going to be gone for a long period of time. So our man was hired for that reason. And so it went.

Arrogance: An Attitude and Way of Life

Now, our shepherd is also a somewhat astute person. He prides himself on being savvy, so he is by no means a simpleton. So here, once again, is his dilemma: Faced with an important and crucial decision to make, he wings it, as arrogance has become part and parcel of his makeup. The arrogance is only on a subtle level — he is not a person you would think of as arrogant, but he did have a small streak of it in him at times. He also thought of himself as a bit of a "know-it-all."

So all of these attributes of his factored into his decision, or lack of decision, did they not? And did not this particular combination of factors, including his personality, attitudes, lifestyle, and "heart-level," contribute to the death of the sheep (and to his death too)? There were even moments further into the story when he could have seen what was happening and made the heartfelt and necessary changes at that moment. But his bit of arrogance regarding the original decision — "I wasn't wrong in the first place," "everything will be okay" — prevented him from changing to a more caring and cautious posture when it was clearly obvious to even the casual observer what the right thing to do would have been. But he continued to maintain that he was right.

So we have our dilemma — and no real way to fix it!

Applying the Principles of the Law of One

How can the principles of the law of one be applied to this story and the others given so far? We have talked about the many moral implications inherent in this parable. The shepherd doesn't seem to care enough to do the right thing by them, but it's not because he's not a good person — it's because he's an *unaware* person. He doesn't live from his heart at all, does he? He goes about his days in what we would call a "heart/sleepwalking fog." He is not awake in his heart yet, is he? So in this unawakened and unaware state, he is living his life only partially, is he not? So when he was faced with a situation that called for him to be more fully awake — awake in his mind and his heart — he was not able to get there. He couldn't see the opportunity for growth, the opportunity to "step up to the plate," wake up, and in that critical and decisive moment, make the decision from both the head and the heart together, could he?

Could it be that he is a little bit like you in some respects? Is there anything about him that you see in yourself? Are you "awake and aware"? If you are, should you be more so, and would you make better and more heart-based decisions if you were? And if you are not yet awake or aware, how can you be if you do not know what it means or what it takes to get there?

17

The Transmuting of Karma: Our Gift from Spirit

The transmuting of karma can be a complex process for some people to understand fully. The way it works is actually a beautiful concept to us of, in your terms, "taking out the garbage." It is the ultimate disposal factory that the Creator has set up to help all people on their path toward ascension to the Infinite, the ultimate goal of humankind — to be reunited with Source. We want to make this an easier process for all to understand, and we want to encourage all to use it often, even every day if necessary.

To understand the law of karma more fully, understand that it is your "reaping and sowing," "good energy/not-good energy" process. Within that, there has been much misunderstanding, but it is merely an operation of balance that can span lifetimes and is there for everyone's benefit, not harm. It is not the barbaric "eye for an eye" of the past — how it was understood in ancient times. The way we understand it is that it is *misqualified* leftover energy that needs to be balanced, forgiven, transmuted, and released. It is a simple process that can be done by anyone at any time.

Now, we realize this may be a huge oversimplification, but the operation is always, in very basic terms, the same. As you deal with dark or "bad" karma, we want you to remember that contained within this construct is darkness, pain, suffering, anger, war, famine, enmity, strife, nonunderstanding, fear, impropriety, murder, torture, and all things evil. (We will talk separately about evil later.)

Also, please realize that not all karma of this type is a person's own. Mass-consciousness karma also exists, but we wanted to inform you of how to transmute individual and group karma, which can be done in the aforementioned prescribed manner.

18

Benjamin Bright

Once upon a time there was a brave little boy named Benjamin Bright. His is a story about family, love, heartache, and triumph. It begins in a distant land long ago but is told as if in present times.

Benjamin, which means "son," was an intelligent, special little boy who had been born into an average family that was typical for the day and time. Benjamin, the youngest, was not like his family at all. They liked to go fishing; he did not. They liked to go hunting for wild game; Benjamin did not. In fact, he didn't like eating meat at all. He preferred much simpler fare — all kinds of vegetables and fruits and nuts. But he was especially fond of squash, potatoes, and pumpkins — he loved pumpkins!

He also loved being in a garden and watching things grow. He found this out because his school planted their own vegetable garden. Ripe tomatoes, yellow crook-necked squash, peppers, green beans, leeks, kale, and pumpkins grew prolifically. How he loved checking on the plants every morning to see how much bigger and faster everything would grow! When the vegetables were harvested, he would count how many pumpkins there were, noticing their different colors and sizes. After that, others started calling him "Benjamin, Benjamin, the Pumpkin Lover" as well as "Benjamin the Bright." He was unfazed by their criticisms and shrugged them off good-naturedly. For you see, Benjamin was born mentally handicapped — just mildly so, but enough that everyone could tell. And despite the whisperings that went on at times, he seemed to love and embrace everyone — and life itself too. There was something truly special about him that people could feel. His mind may have been a bit hampered, but he had a big heart of love for everyone.

His family at first did not know what to do with their mentally challenged child. They were considered a normal family for that time and era, but then here was little Benjamin, so different from them in so many ways. In fact, when they would come home from hunting or fishing trips, he would cry when he saw the dead animals being washed and prepared. So gradually they went on fewer and fewer hunting/fishing expeditions in order to spare little Benjamin's feelings. He loved animals so much that he couldn't bear to see them hurt, much less killed and eaten. His family began a little garden just for him and started growing vegetables, being sure to plant a few pumpkins just for him.

As time went by, Benjamin learned how to work in the family plot to the best of his limited abilities. He learned how to plant, sow, water, and nurture the plants himself. His family eventually got him a pet deer, and some ducks too. They noticed that whenever he was out in the garden or with his animal friends, he seemed like the happiest boy in the world.

Little Benjamin Bright had such a big heart. At first, many people were hesitant around him, but they soon found him to be warm and funny, with a self-deprecating humor and an infectious laugh that put them instantly at ease around him. And so it was that Benjamin Bright was a little boy who was beloved by all. Everywhere he went, it seemed that he was able to bring sunshine into people's lives and hearts.

Now it so happened that he was struck by an illness peculiar to young people with his condition. There was no cure, however, and over a short period of time his health deteriorated and became more and more fragile. The once strong little boy became bound to a sort of wheelchair of that time, but our brave little Benjamin seemed unfazed by it. You could still hear his unique little laugh up and down the hallways of the medical facility. His cheerful attitude and pumpkin pictures pasted on his wheelchair would greet and uplift everyone, including the doctors and nurses who tended him.

However, his health continued to deteriorate, and he begged the doctors to let him go home to be with his family, friends, pets, and beloved pumpkin patch. They let him go, and there he stayed for the rest of his short life. In fact, he was in his garden when he passed away, sitting alone in an alcove in a corner. The sun was shining bright, and it was a beautiful day. Benjamin had been especially happy that day and had told everyone that he wanted to take a nap out in his favorite place, the garden, and that he would be fine.

And so brave little Benjamin fell asleep and never woke up — except, as we know, in heaven. His short but beautiful life was over, but his big heart and ready smile would live forever in people's minds and hearts. He was "Benjamin Bright" after all!

The Nature of Love

We've already told you this sad, but inspiring story, and we've also told you how, in the story, Benjamin triumphed because he had so much love in his heart for everyone. We want to talk about the nature of love, both as it affected Benjamin's life and how it can affect yours, dear readers.

Now, we know that most everyone thinks they know what love is, what it entails and encompasses, and what it is not. But did you also know that you can know and learn what something is by its absence? Do you know what it feels like not to be loved? Unfortunately, many people do. Because, you see … when we talk about the law of karma in regard to love, what do we mean? Here is what *we* mean: Our interpretation of it is that all karma is due either to love or to a lack of love. Do you see, dear readers?

So in our story of the sheep and the shepherd, everything bad that happened could be traced back to a basic lack of love. The shepherd failed to "love" the sheep — he didn't really care about them — and that's what then incurred the karma, the sin, was it not? And when the shepherd still failed to care — love — even after the first sheep was killed, he sealed his own fate, didn't he? It was simply and basically due to a lack of love.

Now let's take a look at a different situation. In our original hare story, what about the building of the waste plant too close to the hare community? I think that we can admit that, at some point, there was some disconnect going on with the site selection committee. Apparently the presence of the large community of rabbits in (relatively) close proximity to the plant didn't concern them much — at least not enough to change the site of the plant's construction to a different location. So here again we have a lack of appropriate concern, do we not? A lack of love.

Now let's look at love from the opposite perspective. Let's go ahead and look at the Benjamin Bright story. Here we have a mentally challenged child with a heart so big that he literally transforms the people around him. He challenges them to dig deep within themselves and be better than they might have been normally. The extra patience, time and care required for an individual like Benjamin stretches even the best of us, but we are better people for it, are we not, dear readers? You could say, then, that his tremendous heart of love melted and transformed even the most hardened hearts of those around him, did it not? The love he gave enhanced his world and everyone around him. This is an excellent example of the healing power of love, is it not? The karma here is in its positive mode. As we said, all karma is due either to love or to a lack of it. It's really quite simple when you look at it that way.

The Law of One: A Foundation of Love

So how does this hearken back to the law of one, as mentioned earlier in the book? When we talked about the law of one, we talked about it as a prelude to this book. One of its main tenets is the foundational power of love — how it undergirds everything in and concerning it. It literally *is* the foundation. Do you not think that there is love out there in the universe on other planets? *There is!* It is not only the foundation of everything here on Earth — it is the foundation of all life "out there" too!

From the creation of the universe to the teeming life on the millions of planets out there — yes, millions! — the Creator imbued all things with love, and indeed, life could not exist without love, neither here on Earth nor out in the universe at large. There are not worlds out there like the planet Vulcan in the *Star Trek* series, because you cannot have a planet or a great civilization not founded on — or where its people do not or cannot feel — love. The beings on such a planet would die out, for the simple fact that life and love are interchangeable: **Love = life = love = life = love.** You see the point.

So what we are saying here is that the law of karma is based on love — or the lack of love! The law of one could not operate without love; it is as simple as that. Love equals life equals love!

19

New Beginnings

The beginning of this story marks the anniversary of a fledgling civilization in Egypt many, many eons ago. It was actually before the Great Pyramid was built, in a time period called *Juemen eiueik L-Mae-oi'uae-Mu sek le* in the ancient Lemurian language, which is no longer spoken on Earth. Back in that time and place, there lived two men who met later in their lives and had a tremendous and lasting effect on each other, changing the directions of their lives and of the world at that time.

We will tell you about the first one, whose (unpronounceable) name was *Ten ey* C' *teanta*, but we will call him T for short to make it easier for you, dear reader. Now T was raised in a small hamlet in Lemuria by very loving parents. He received the best education that a child of that time could get, one to which the whole large family group, or clan, contributed. Each child of that time had the benefit of this education and knew and loved each member of the clan. The children not only got the benefits of their parents' love and wisdom, but they were lucky enough to receive gifts from everyone.

Now, our boy T was found to be very psychically gifted, so after this was discovered, extra special care was taken to instruct him in how to use his gifts lovingly and wisely and always think of others as equal to himself. He was taught how to meditate at a very young age and developed superbly on what would be called, in our modern age, a yogic path. When T got older, he was able to sit at the feet of the masters of the Lemurian culture, whose high vibrations and love for all things permeated and helped shape their illustrious civilization.

Now, T was living in what would unfortunately be called the end times for Lemuria. When he became a man, something very sad and tragic was about to happen; the great seers and psychics of Lemuria had intuited the nefarious energy/ideas of their would-be attackers, the ones who wanted to annihilate them, before it happened. A warning went out that whoever wanted to leave should do so immediately, so ships were made ready for the long journey. They knew there were large continents to the west and east of them, so different ships were sent out for the new land. They all knew, too, that these trips would be long and that they would not be able to go back — ever. It was a very sad time for all, for it meant that they would be giving up all that they had built up for literally thousands of years.

However, much of the populace refused to believe the warnings. They simply could not believe that anything or anybody could be dastardly enough to try to destroy them, so in their naiveté and disbelief, they stayed. But those who realized what could happen made quick but thorough preparations and left. T was one of those who had intuited the thoughts and images of the impending destruction. He tried in vain to convince his clan members, his personal family, to come with him, but some said that even if such a terrible thing were to happen, they wanted to stay anyway. They just could not bear to leave!

Now, the ones leaving made sure to bring certain items, tools, and accouterments of their society, but they did not need very many material things, for, you see, each one carried the knowledge of the culture within themselves. The principles of the civilization were inscribed in the hearts and minds of each and every Lemurian so they could rebuild their culture, if need be.

And so the great ships went off in many different directions, and the Lemurians took their culture, their language, and their ways of living and thinking around the globe. Shortly after their departure, Lemuria was indeed hit by many cataclysms, both from the air and from the resulting earthquakes and floods that sank the thousands of large and small islands that comprised it. In the end all was sunk, and the great civilization that had lasted for over 100,000 years was lost. As for the few islands that were left, a rising sea claimed them eventually too.

The Lemurians Arrive in Egypt

Except for the travelers in their ships, all would have been lost, but the ship that T was on made its way to what is now called Egypt. They landed there and had brought their Lemurian ideals of family and culture with them. T helped in the setting up of a temple complex and was highly instrumental in establishing schools of all kinds in order to teach and hand down the great Lemurian tenets of his former life and culture. When they landed, they met and intermingled with the native culture already there, and Egypt began to grow and advance very rapidly, especially in those early years.

Now, the people of Lemuria all lived very long lives, due in large part to the presence of a thing called "the firmament" — huge sheets of ice set in place in the upper stratosphere that blocked the harmful UV rays from the Sun. This allowed them to be extraordinarily healthy, as it allowed the thymus gland to expand, which gave them the ability to live hundreds of years instead of only decades.

So our man T, due to his extremely long life, was able to guide and nurture the new Lemurian civilization of Egypt for some 300–400 years. With his extraordinary mind and abilities, his guidance was integral to the establishment of the new Lemuria. But we are getting too far ahead of ourselves in the story. Wait until he meets Geoueao'e'i L'eaieoutkl E' maeou'i — G!

When the voyagers from Lemuria landed in Egypt at that time in Earth history, there was, as we said, a group of native Egyptians living there. When the Lemurians landed, the majority of the Egyptians had not heard of the land of Lemuria. But the new people were quite friendly and nice, and they were certainly not the conquering type at all.

G Meets the Lemurians

Among the Egyptians was a young man named Geoueao'e, whom we will call G for short. He was a bright young man, very smart for his age and the limiting culture that he grew up in, and he was eager for adventure. But he was a little bit sad because he knew that he would probably never get to travel. So he had resigned himself to the simple life he had at the time, because his culture was so basic and relatively primitive. But then these new people arrived from somewhere far away. G was exhilarated and ran to the landing place to greet them.

He stood back at first as they unloaded, and he heard them speak in a language that he had not heard before. Looking around, he noticed that there was a man only slightly older than him — not by much — who seemed to be in charge. They deferred to him at times, and G saw him giving orders, but in a very friendly, courteous, and kind way. G noticed that these new people helped each other a great deal and didn't seem to have that much that they brought with them, which was unusual. The young man in charge looked around and saw G standing there, watching. The young man in charge — T, of course — walked over to G and tried to communicate with him. Using hand gestures, T asked G if he could find a water source and where he and the Lemurians could set up temporary lodging. Pointing and gesturing also, G showed him where to find water and where they could live for a while. G tried to ask T where he and his people were from, and "Lemuria" is what he was told. T tried to explain about the destruction of his home, but G was not sure what he was saying.

The first night on dry land was a relief for the weary voyagers, for it had been a long, long journey. And little by little, each culture started learning the language of the other. And as the Egyptians heard the story of the Lemurians, they were at once fascinated and appalled that any civilization so advanced and so beautiful could ever have been beset upon by anyone. G had not heard of Lemuria, but a few of the elders had heard that two distant civilizations lived on two different sides of the world, but these had just been unconfirmed rumors. G and the other Egyptians were amazed at what the Lemurians told them and eventually started to teach them.

T and G Become Friends

G was born in the Nile delta area of prehistoric Egypt. He had a limited education and had only worked in the farm fields and rich marshes surrounding the delta area. T, on the other hand, had come as a survivor of a beautiful civilization, Lemuria, that was now gone. But T, as we told you, had an advantaged, loving, and advanced upbringing and education. All of this — plus his extraordinary apprenticeship years — had built up his natural abilities to the point that, in spite of his relatively young age, people sought advice from him and placed him in roles of authority.

So here was the meeting and merging of two vastly different cultures. The Egyptians taught the newcomers how to live in their region of the world and how to farm the delta, and the newcomers taught the Egyptians all about Lemurian life and culture; one enhanced the other and vice versa.

G and T became great friends. T found out that this interesting young man who was close in age to him had an avid and eager mind for learning. He was able to teach G many things about the Lemurian culture and how to preserve its principles in order to re-found and rebuild the civilization again. T and G learned each other's languages and enjoyed conversing in both. As we told you, they became fast friends. T even taught G meditation techniques, and G learned how to apply them daily and started to advance.

But to G, the most fascinating and heartfelt thing was how much love, respect, and cooperation he observed within each Lemurian family/clan unit, and how the children, especially, thrived within them. He liked how much care was taken with each child, and how each child's innate abilities were assessed very early by the spiritually advanced members of each community, which enabled them to give each child individual guidance early on that brought out their talents and enabled them to strengthen innate weaknesses — all with proper and great care to allow time for play, exploration, creativity, and the discovery of the natural world. G's own upbringing had left a lot to be desired. He also found, to his great surprise, that it wasn't always the parents who raised the children. The person or persons in the clan who had the best and most loving parenting skills and the specific skills that each child would need, usually a group of wise and mature individuals, would raise and guide the child to maturation. This was definitely different from how G was raised, but he grew to appreciate how much smarter, talented, and happier the children raised this way were. This was just one example of the advancement of the Lemurian civilization. There were many more.

The History behind the Men's Powerful Friendship

Our two men, T and G, were so dissimilar, were they not? T was very high minded and advanced, even for a Lemurian. He embraced love, light, and wisdom and was a model for enlightenment. G, on the other hand, had grown up disadvantaged but had managed to work hard to remold and reshape his life as he matured. T had given him, and modeled for him, a goal in life, something to work toward and strive for. His naturally adventurous spirit had blossomed and turned inward. He discovered he was adventurous and creative, even courageous, in the inner levels. His growing and rich inner life transformed his outer life in ways that he couldn't have imagined. His outer life gradually began to reflect the inner, and his own inner light and love began to glow like a light bulb suddenly supplied with a stronger battery.

The two men cared for and admired each other greatly. Theirs was a powerful friendship. They did not know the reason why they became such close friends so quickly, but we do: G and T had known each other before in a previous life when they were the two daughters of a fisherman.

They were both tomboys growing up, and their father had trained them to sail boats, even though at the time girls were not usually allowed to do "men" things. But after their mother died, the father indulged them and secretly trained them so that they could all be together. You see, the girls were twins, and their mother had died in childbirth, so their papa had raised them more like boys. Late one day, however, they were out on their great lake — which was more like an inland sea — when a mighty storm blew in. Their sturdy but relatively small ship was engulfed by huge waves. Their father was on deck trying to secure the sails when he was pitched overboard. The two girls screamed and cried at the sudden loss of their father, but both ran over to secure the mast and sail. Clinging to each other for strength and comfort, they managed to weather out the storm. When dawn broke and the clouds started to clear, using the skills that their father had taught them, they managed to navigate their way back to land safely.

There in their hometown, they put up a headstone for their father right next to their mother's. For the rest of that lifetime, they never married but remained each other's best friends for their whole long lives.

When they met again in this present life, they both felt the strong bond of their previous sojourn, so even though they were from totally different backgrounds and had grown up thousands of miles away from each other, the good energy of the old relationship rekindled. They both liked each other instantly, and they eventually found out why.

In their previous life together, T and G were anchors for each other. They were there for each other. When they met this time, the nature of their past relationship reawakened and rekindled old feelings of love, loyalty, and respect that they had for each other that were brought forward into their present relationship. Now relationships, even good ones, still need work, but some relationships tend to be easier than others because many of the bugs have already been worked out previously, and T and G's relationship had that quality to it.

Each One Complemented the Other

We have talked about what T was able to give G, but what we haven't talked about are G's talents and abilities. G had always had a knack for growing things. Even as a very young boy, anything he would plant in his garden just grew wonderfully — he really had a green thumb! His tomatoes and peppers were always the biggest and best ones, and his flowers were lush and beautiful. He had a great gift: that of being close to the earth and the land. He just seemed as if he had a real connection with it, and it responded to his care.

T, on the other hand, knew next to nothing about growing things, as he was a more etheric and cerebral type of person, always kind of up in the air. G provided a great contrast to T; one was in his head all the time, and one was very grounded, so each one complemented the other. Together, they balanced each other well.

So when T began to rise in the hierarchy of the new Lemuria, G was right there with him — a best friend in all circumstances. T would have something important to talk about and then they would talk. G provided a good sounding board for T and told him frankly what he thought. And sometimes they would just have to agree that they disagreed, but the respect was always there, and they would continue to talk things out. So their relationship stayed healthy and strong.

T had brought some things with him from Lemuria. Even as a child, he loved to play with rocks, stones, and crystals. He had many different stones, but the ones that he brought were silicon crystals. These crystals resonated with him and were filled with his meditation energy. When he took one particular stone out, he held it in his hand and it glowed. T felt the energy of his homeland in it and felt melancholy, but he also felt strengthened in the knowledge that his civilization had not been totally destroyed — because they all carried Lemuria in their hearts!

Most everything that the Lemurians did was different from what the native Egyptians were accustomed to. At first, the native Egyptians were not sure what to think of the new ways, but like G, when they saw the principles in action and saw how easily and well they worked, they started to open their minds to adapt to the better way. Various ways of industry, including the building of waterways and eventually the building of the Great Pyramid itself, were taught to the people of Egypt of that time and place.

T was, as we said, a natural-born leader, and with G by his side to help him, he was able to accomplish great things. He helped to establish the great mystery schools where meditative techniques and soundwave technology were first used. The Lemurians' greatest skills lay in the love they had in their hearts for all things, but they were also good at weaving, pottery, and metallurgy. They were not so superior in physical inventions insomuch as their expertise lay in their knowledge and connection with the inner realms of what is now called mysticism. In that day and age, however, it was pure and very high in vibration. It was considered a science, and these spiritual techniques and knowledge were shared, used, and taught.

The Lemurian Credo of Existence

The Lemurians' tremendous metaphysical abilities and talents were highly advanced; they were very in tune with the beautiful, many-layered inner realms of existence. High-minded and spiritual is what you would call them now, and T excelled in those particular things. In his mind and soul, he brought the heart of Lemuria to Egypt and, with many others, planted it there deep within the soil, deep within the consciousness of the world at that time. He was able to teach these spiritual techniques and the Lemurian credo of existence to all who were there. They benefitted greatly from his teachings and expertise. T wanted to make a civilization based on Lemurian principles that would endure for an eternity. His intent was that what happened to Lemuria would never happen again on planet Earth.

G was a very apt pupil and learned so much from T that he was later able to teach the Egyptian people, those who were ready to learn, the advanced techniques of meditation and the high principles of metaphysics. G and T worked together with certain groups of people, but G worked more with the indigenous Egyptians, some of whom were ready and some of whom were not, but enough of them did learn the ways of the Lemurians and were able to greatly benefit from them.

Embedded deep within the Lemurian credo of existence were the principles of the law of one, which they had received from many, many different people and civilizations from the different star systems with which they had been in constant contact for many millennia. The world of the Lemurian empire at that time was an intergalactic system of government that was based on individual self-government, thereby eliminating the need for an overall central government. The wonderful, wise, and good people of Lemuria did not need any of these things. Within such an intergalactic empire, every person, every citizen, policed themselves and lived the high principles in which they believed. They not only believed in these things, but they were taught from babyhood onward that this was the type of person to be.

The young children of Lemuria were guided and instructed by very loving members of the clan in how to be loving, caring, unselfish, hardworking, and responsible people who learned not only how to take care of themselves and each other, but how to care for, take care of, and appreciate the natural world around them from day one. They simply were taught that all is one, and that they were integrally part of that oneness. The beauty and majesty of the natural world was considered a precious entity to be loved and appreciated and taken care of, if need be. They were taught that each planet was beautiful in its own right and provided them a home, and that they were to treat that home with as much concern and consideration as they treated each other. No child or person who was a citizen of Lemuria would have ever even thought to hurt or harm any part of nature.

Even their dwellings reflected a respect and honor for the needs of their mother, Earth. Earth at that time had a very stable and balmy climate. Most of the world at that time was subtropical and had an even temperature year-round, so most Lemurians lived in very simple dwellings that were open-air and had minimal, if any, negative impact on the environment or the ecosystem of the area. Some even lived in caves and had underground houses in order to blend in as a way of respecting the beauty and fragility of the areas where they lived. There was, however, a large complex in the center of the larger grouping of islands in the approximate center of the Lemurian "continent," but this had been built in an area where the impact on the ecosystems from the construction was minimal, if any. Large waterways were also built in cooperation with, and with the full knowledge of, the bodies of water that were being affected.

Lemurians of that time and place could communicate with all of nature, and they never did anything without consulting and communicating with the devic spirits or the consciousness of a particular region of Earth. As Mother Earth and the devic spirits were consulted and approval was obtained, they would assist and guide the builders in every aspect of any construction — such as where the best areas were for a project — and they were kept in the loop and consulted at every turn.

The Law of One

We know that this last part will be a difficult concept for our readers to wrap their heads around, but we are simply trying to give you the facts of the way things were done, and why they were done that way, in ancient Lemuria.

The Lemurians took the credos of the law of one very seriously and lived them every day. It was a set of principles that carried with it a sacredness equivalent to every one of the sacred books that are currently used as moral guidelines in modern societies around the world. In Lemuria they had one — the law of one — and it informed everything they did, and everything they thought about, and it was intimately involved in every decision, every action, every project, and every moment of every day. It was written in the hearts and minds of every Lemurian and was taught to their children from day one. So complete and so good were these tenets of living that no other guide was needed or ever even thought of as necessary! They had inherited the law of one from the star systems that had seeded them, and it was of such superior quality and had worked for countless millennia on other planet systems, so there was never any question or thought otherwise of using or needing any other kind of guidance — the law of one was *the* guide, and all that was ever necessary.

Their great civilization lived in harmony and oneness with all things, including each other. Animals, plants, water, earth — all were considered to be brothers in creation and equal partners in everything and with every decision, so much so that all their lives were symbiotic in their very nature and inception. The needs of all concerned were always considered in an equal way one to another. No one's needs were ever considered to be more important than another's. That is one reason why the water spirits and the water itself were considered, consulted, and involved in every decision of the project mentioned above. The people of Lemuria simply would not have dreamed of doing things any other way, because the law of one means that all are one — you are me, and I am you — and it can be no other way, for that is the greater reality, and that truly, truly *is* the way things are!

, , ,

We of the Sirian Council of 12 give this great work to the people of Earth in hopes that by giving our readers concrete examples of Lemurian life, or parables and stories showing the principles of the law of one in action or non-action, we can inform and help the people of Earth to appreciate the larger picture — how the law of one operates and could be used in full implementation on this planet.

We have endeavored with the Lemurian story to show you that, indeed, the law of one has already been here and in use on this planet for untold thousands of years; it worked well and informed one of the greatest civilizations that was ever here! The Lemurian civilization lasted for much longer than your scientists would ever believe, acknowledge, or appreciate. The Lemurian culture and civilization lasted for more than 100,000 years before it was sunk and destroyed by the combined forces of evil and nature.

For now and for always, please know that we wish to gift this to you and bring you into the new age and the twenty-first century with a new legacy for your civilization and your lives. We bring you the galactic unified law of one!

20

On Death and Dying

We want you all to know that we understand and honor the tremendous grief that is associated with the process of someone dying. Everyone is loved by someone, and we know it is a difficult subject to even talk about for a lot of you. We want to be very careful how we say this so that you all will understand the process of someone who is ready to pass. Please don't misunderstand us here. There is not one of us in this Group who has not experienced this, so we have great compassion and understanding for what people on Earth think and feel concerning these issues.

It is our understanding that most people here actually believe that death is real. They try to believe in the hereafter, but for many of you, this is such a gray area because you believe that your loved one is going into a void of nothingness. Nobody quite believes the rather naïve — and may we say silly? — story of angels floating around with harps and singing hymns all day in heaven, or the existence of a heavenly gate with Saint Peter standing there taking roll call on a never-ending scroll. We think most people *hope* that they or their loved ones are going to heaven, and they do, but the old, tired picture of harps and angels floating about in heaven — that *is* true, but it is much different, and much better than that.

So here's what we're going to do: We're going to try to describe heaven for you to let you know where you or your loved ones will most likely go at the time of passing. There is a realm (not a physical place) called "the ethers" that everyone starts out in before they come to Earth (incarnate), and when life in the physical is over — meaning life here on Earth — they return to the ethers until they come back (reincarnate) again.

The Wheel of Samsara

In Eastern philosophy, the cycle of birth, death, and rebirth is called *the wheel of samsara*, and it represents the "birth, death, rebirth" process as moving in a circle from birth to death to rebirth. In this analogy, it operates like a wheel turning, going around and around, which is a pretty accurate picture of this eternal cycle. A person comes into incarnation from the ethers (heaven), then back again in death into the ethers from where they came, then back into the physical (rebirth), and so on. It keeps repeating itself until the person is spiritually ready for the release from the Earth cycles, which is called the "ascension."

Every person on Earth is here working and moving toward that goal; refining, improving, and hopefully moving forward; learning and applying spiritual principles, hoping in some lifetime to advance toward the attainment of the cessation of the cycle. A person may get off of the wheel of samsara through personal efforts and the sincere application of spiritual principles. This is the ultimate goal of each and every human in incarnation upon this planet!

Now that we have explained the overall process of the life-death-life cycle, there is something that we need all of you to understand: *There is no death ever!* No soul ever truly perishes. The process of "death" is the physical transit of the body only; it goes to sleep and the spirit leaves the physical body — which, by the way, is a very beautiful process of its own. It's like birth in reverse.

We want everyone to get this part. Read it, and write it in your hearts and minds: *There is no death!* Please believe us when we tell you this. This is the true reality, the way it really is. Put aside your older belief systems and replace them with this. It is what your beloved Jeshua (Jesus) was trying to leave with you. It is the beautiful message of the ascension. It was not only real for him, but it is real for you — all of you — too! Please do not ever question this. It is a fact!

Now, as to the question of what the "death" experience is actually like, we would like to give a description of what usually happens when a person passes. Imagine, if you will, a person who has been ill for a long time. This person knows she is getting ready to move on because she starts to feel different. That different feeling is the soul starting to exit when the moment is close. The way that it leaves the body is out through the top of the head. So when the moment arrives, there is a release by the proper body of the source of the life *indwelling* it.

So gently, slowly, the spirit/soul starts lifting away from the physical body, but it does this starting from the feet and moving upward, so it is not lifting horizontally — it is lifting vertically. It comes slowly up — but sometimes it has to come fast! — as each of the body's energy centers lets go and retracts from it. In Sanskrit, these energy centers are called chakras (pronounced *shaw-kras*). The feet chakras let go first and then so on up the body.

Now, the soul actually has an energy "body" that extends below the feet, and there is a chakra below the feet that keeps you anchored here on Earth. So in reality, the Earth chakra lets go first. Now this is profound — I hope you all realize — because at birth each and every one of you put down your roots into the realm of Earth, and while you are on Earth in physicality, you are connected to her. So in the "death" process, Earth lets go and releases you. Then all the feet chakras start to release and retract from the soul, which is rising. As it moves upward through the physical body, then, as each chakra releases, the person who is passing can feel this process, and there is usually little or no resistance to it. This whole process takes between two and five minutes, depending on the individual and the circumstance. In cases of sudden death, however, the soul sometimes has no choice but to exit much faster than is normal — sometimes in a matter of seconds, if it has to! This is a tremendous shock to these people, who will end up floating in the air above the scene, traumatized and wondering what just happened. In their minds, one moment they were driving, or whatever they were doing, and then the next moment they're floating in the air above their lifeless body at the scene.

We want all of you, dear readers, to know that the soul of a person *is* that person — you are not a physical body at all. You only live in one for the duration of each lifetime. So when we tell you that the "person" is floating overhead, we mean it. It's just that the person was usually in his or her body but now is out of it.

It is always important to send lots of prayers to and for someone who just made the transition, especially if the death was sudden or unexpected, because that person is in shock and great sadness at being abruptly thrown out of his or her body. And as such people probably had not prepared themselves for this probability, the finality of their passing can be a difficult adjustment for some. Some people are angry, and some people feel cheated. Some just miss their loved ones so much because they didn't want to leave so soon. We sometimes get so caught up in our own grief that we can forget that those who have "died" are probably sad too. But for a person who has been ill for a long time, or for the elderly, death can be a relief, and they are glad to be moving on. And many, many people can feel the heavenly ethers before they pass.

Finally, we want to tell you that there is no need to fear death. It is as natural as life itself. Please feel comforted that your loved ones are in a good place where they can rest and recharge their batteries, a place where they can take all the time they need to look over their lives they just left, and learn what they did right and what they did wrong so that they can make proper choices when they are ready — hopefully not immediately — to come back here into physicality again for the next go-round.

There are a few rare souls who get lost when they exit and can wander around as ghosts. This is a very sad plight for any soul, and sometimes a person does not realize that they've passed on. For example, if someone died in his sleep and "got up" the next morning, he may not realize that he's moved on. The ethers "over there" are very real, and that's a discussion that we will leave for another time.

When you are getting ready to pass, whether through illness, old age, or something else, the process we just described is going to happen with you. You may or may not feel it coming. Many people do, but just as many do not. It does not matter either way. Days before — or for others, weeks before — the actual day, the body starts its process, very slowly at first, called *retraction*. It starts withdrawing itself from the indwelling spirit/soul, and how it does this is by starting to put something called the "body battery" to sleep.

It gradually, slowly, starts retracting energy from the body cells and energy centers, the chakras. There is a pulling back from the cells and the chakras, and the life energy for that incarnation starts ebbing lower and lower, a bit like a battery or a flashlight, fading lower and lower. It is very gradual at first, but as the moment approaches, the process starts accelerating.

Now, on an energetic or physical level, you may or may not feel something going on. You may have a sense that something's different but you can't pinpoint it. Some people feel the subtle energy changes, and some people do not; it is a very individual thing. There is no right or wrong here — only the way it is.

Let's take you, for example, and let's say that you don't sense anything until a day or two before. And then all of a sudden you have no energy for no apparent reason at all. Then, when you stop your busy day and take a breather, you realize that something feels different — kind of an odd, funny feeling. It's not pain, exactly, but you suddenly realize that something's not right. Now, let's say you are about to have a massive heart attack, and in that moment you think that maybe you should go to the doctor or the emergency room. This is a situation in which the death process can be halted. Say you go to the ER, and after a few hours they put you on the heart monitor. They find out that your cholesterol is sky-high and your major arteries are 80 to 90 percent blocked, and you didn't know it. You never had any symptoms, but there is the evidence on the machine. So they take you to surgery and do an emergency triple bypass on you, and you survive. This is one of the few instances where a death process can be reversed if the physical things leading to it are caught in time.

Let's say that you feel funky, but you dismiss it totally and go to bed then back to work the next day. You did not recognize that your body was getting ready to pass on, and that day the moment arrives. It's so quick and sudden that you end up floating above your body, wondering what happened.

So those are two sides of the coin of a similar scenario. One results in a complete reversal of the death process, where retraction stops and energy starts flowing to recharge the body battery. That person — you — gets to live longer in physicality (here).

Looking at side two of that same coin, and now you have just passed over — and here's the kicker: You're still alive, but your soul exited out the top of your head, and your incarnation is over. The life that was "you," inhabiting and indwelling your body, is now just you! You are now in your original spirit form, and have returned to the ethers where you were before you were born.

Now let's take another scenario. Let's say that you are very elderly and you've been sick for a long time. You're ready to go. You have felt the retraction of your physical body and felt your energy ebbing lower and lower for a week or two, maybe more. So you know death is imminent, and you welcome it. The moment finally arrives, and you embrace it.

At the moment of passing, you feel the energy start to leave your feet. Then you feel it drawing up past your knees. You take a couple of deep breaths and relax. You go with it and offer no resistance. Then, a minute or two later, you feel "yourself" only in the upper chest and head area. You say your goodbyes to the loved ones around you and take your last breath. Feeling a pulling sensation, your soul — you — slips out through a place in the center of the top of your head, and you feel totally at peace. You hover for a moment over your body lying there on the bed, take one last lingering look at your former self, and you say goodbye to your family and friends from your heart/mind and mind/heart. Then you feel that powerful pulling sensation again, as if you are being drawn back through a birth canal of the ethers — heaven.

At this point, you are experiencing the strong pull of going from one dimension to a higher one than you just left. As you are being pulled, you feel such a sense of pure unconditional love coming from the Godhead welcoming you back! On the other side, "deceased" friends and relatives greet you, and you all have one big celebration party! Everyone pats you on the back, saying, "Welcome back," "We haven't seen you in a long time," and so on. You can envision the picture in your mind.

So, you just had a peaceful and beautiful experience, did you not? You were ready to go and transited well — and easily. This last "you" was a perfect example of the kind of death experience many of you actually will have. Death is not a bad thing to be feared or avoided, but a graceful soul/energy transition from this life to the next.

We want to leave you with this thought from the channel, as she has a beautiful way to sum this up for all of you:

"Your death from heaven was your birth into this life, and your death from this life is your birth into heaven!"

21

Love and the Law of One

We have been talking about love and the law of one and how that applies to the lessons of humanity's dealings with each other and its world. What we see happening here, on a very large scale because there are so many of you now, is a general lack of love in regard to your planet, Earth. We know that it is not out of intentionality that Earth is being hurt; it is more in the way of unintentionality. The reason why we put the shepherd story toward the end is because we are trying to get through to people about the *laissez-faire* attitude toward Earth that still pervades much of the planet's population. You see, your Earth is at a breaking point right now in its evolution as a planet, so we are going to continue in that vein for a little while longer, if you will bear with us.

The Old-Fashioned Bucket

Imagine, if you will, that Earth is like an old-fashioned bucket sitting out back under a constantly dripping waterspout. In our illustration, the water has been shut off, but it is an old water faucet, and there's this little leak — not much, but a constant *drip, drip, drip*. Each drop is not that much and quite tiny in comparison to the bucket, which is large, but as any plumber or water company will tell you, a constantly dripping faucet can leak many gallons before someone realizes it and fixes the faucet.

So in our analogy, your Earth is like the bucket. She, if we may call Earth "she," is big and old and still beautiful! But imagine, if you will, that the dripping faucet is the people living on Earth, and the water drops are not really water drops, but trash, garbage, plastic bottles, and sewage that keep dripping away constantly in a never-ending, constant flow. You are beginning to get the picture.

Most people do not think in terms of the bigger picture when it comes to disposing of trash, industrial solvents and waste, air pollution, and so on. But in the past thirty years or so, many of you have become much more aware that your personal "stuff" affects the larger picture, the point of which is this: Our Earth is now at such a critical point with our pollution that her bucket is starting to overflow — she just cannot hold and dispose of it quickly enough, and she is weakened and growing more ill every day.

Now, we want to thank everyone who *is* aware and those who *are* doing their best to help. We applaud and appreciate you very much for your efforts and what is being done. But it is still not quite enough. Earth needs everyone around the world to find better ways of disposal.

Let's All Get on Board

What we are trying to do in this chapter is ask *all* of you to please get on board with this. As another analogy, think of your Earth as a nest — your home. Now, think of the television program that shows houses so cluttered and dirty that they have become almost unlivable. Then think of how spacious, beautiful, and inviting the house becomes after everything has been disposed of, after the house has been restored to its original luster, cleanliness, and beauty. So if Earth is our home, would we dirty it? Or would we want to try a little harder to maintain and appreciate it? Yes, we think that most people would want to keep up with the trash and help keep and maintain the home for future generations to come — our children, our children's children, and so on.

So please — wherever you are in the world when you are reading this, take a look around and see if improvements could be made in the local area, town, or country where you live. Be bold and ask your local governments to work harder on improving what they are already doing. Let's get everybody on board here! The Earth needs ALL of us, not just some of us, to be aware every day of where the trash is going.

Smart People to the Rescue: A Clarion Call

If you are a company and your waste goes down the river, it still goes someplace on Earth, doesn't it? "Out of sight" is not "out of mind" when it comes to waste disposal. In business and industry, there are some brilliant minds out there — think of a better solution! Like the shepherd in the story in this book, you simply have to *care enough* to do something about it.

Make no mistake — your planet is on the brink of dying. Her oceans, her rivers, her air — there is so much now that her poor "bucket" cannot hold any more. She is not only overflowing; she is starting to break apart! Rust and filth are destroying everything, as they always do. Let's give her some breathing room, shall we?

Now, we know there are some exciting new technologies that have been created and are coming along — use them! Since you are all in the bucket, and you are all creating the drops, let's stop *your drop* in some way — let's find a way! If you're doing something but it's not really working that well, then let's rethink and rework it. You all have so much potential, drive, and brain power that is not being used.

We Care — Do You?

What we are trying to say here is — and we know we've gone off on a tangent here — get off your couches and do something. Do something to help every day, if you can, or at least every weekend. Maybe a little less partying and a little more caring would help Earth a lot! (Whew!)

Well, now that we've said our piece, we hope that you all will think more on this and make some changes. Remember, you don't want to be the shepherd who doesn't really care — you want to be the caring, good shepherd who takes better care of his flock, his fields, and his world!

Why? Because he simply *cares!*

22

Familial Integrity — Our Gift

We have our major themes already thoroughly delineated, such as the laws of unity, love, diversity in unity, harmony, balance, will, and such topics that we have discussed at quite some length. Many of the stories are anecdotal and whimsical when they start, and then, dear readers, as you know well by now, they unexpectedly swerve into the fast lane and take you on a different journey than you were expecting. Isn't that right? Other stories are in this book simply to show the power of love, brotherhood, sacrifice, and balance, and the value of not giving up on yourself.

We of the Sirian Council of 12 give this book to all humankind as a gift to give you the specifics and the overview necessary for your planet and your civilization to survive, flourish, advance, and take its place among the great planets of this galaxy and beyond. We of your sister planet starseeded yours long ago. The message we wish to convey to the people of Earth is this: Know that we love you and have watched over you, lived with you, suffered with you, and rejoiced with you. We are from another planet, yes, but we are far from being aliens. We are your older brothers and sisters in the light, and we see that you are ready, dear people of Earth, to move forward. You are ready for the next big step, and this is it. It is a piece of the beginning of your New Earth!

You are all ascending in various ways on your planet, as is your Earth Mother. She is indeed in travail at this very moment and needs your help, your collective help, desperately! We cannot stress this enough nor minimize the role that you must all play in restoring her to balance and homeostasis. She will do what she has to do to stabilize herself, and she is trying very hard to hurt as few of you as possible. You should know that many lightworkers around the planet have been working overtime for years too.

Please — we love you all very much, but your inattention to Earth's signals and your failure to address certain key problems has made it more difficult than it had to be. Please be aware that people who do not have to are dying on your planet every day! We just need more of you to *care*, actually care, about the other people, creatures, plant life, and so on.

You are at a critical point where your Mother Earth needs more people to be involved in helping her. She needs large numbers of you using all your resources and everything you have at your disposal along with your great capacity for invention, your ingenuity, and your diligence to be turned toward her right now. She needs your talents, your time, your genius, and most of all your love!

You have a tremendous capacity for love. We know — we helped seed you with that long ago. Creation started with love from the great Creator, and only love can save your planet now! You and Earth are all in this together, and we want you to learn to honor and respect her more. Don't spit on her with industrial waste and things that you know will hurt her. These types of things can be neutralized or even used by other species of your world. Again, we urge you: Do not delay or defer these solutions any longer! We have watched the pollution of your beautiful planet both from afar and from right here with you, and we can no longer remain silent. We wish for you, the people of Earth, to have a beautiful home in which to live for many eons to come, and we see two futures for you hanging in the balance:

1) One in which an environmentally crippled planet limps into its future, just barely hanging on at all, or …

2) One in which Earth has recovered her pristine beauty, environmental health, and balance and can easily sustain and provide a nest for all forms of life on her!

Which do you think you are headed for, and how can you be part of the solution — her solution *and your own?*

23

Tribute to Lily

We are here to bring greetings and welcome to you from the Sirian Council of 12. We want to tell you a bit about Lily himself, as we are not sure that a "bio" of him has ever been given.

Lily was originally a Sirian officeholder of a type you would term freemasonry. He was a member of the high council of that elite organization here on our planet of Sirius B many, many of your years ago. Lily, of course, is not his real name. He prefers to be known by this term of Lily in your culture because the lily represents beauty, exquisite form, and perfection, and the thousand-petaled lily/lotus represents cosmic consciousness. The lily of the valley in your culture also has a meaning of sacredness. And lastly, your beloved Jeshua talked about their purity, abundance, and freedom: "Consider the lilies of the field, how they grow; they toil not, neither do they spin: And yet I say unto you, That even Solomon in all his glory was not arrayed like one of these" (Matt 6:28-30, *KJV*). This is a reference to the abundance of God, the trust, and the beautiful divine quality of the love that the Infinite has for us all!

Lily sincerely wanted this flower to represent his presence in your world, as it represents the qualities that he both has and exudes. In our culture he was a tower of virtue, strength, wisdom, and leadership, and he represents some of the best that our culture has to offer another. Make no mistake — he is as God-filled and love-filled as Jeshua, Kuthumi, or any being or angelic presence being channeled in your culture today. The channel can feel his presence and his energy coming alive and springing forth from the pages of this book — each character, each story, each imaginative, glorious purpose put to form and paper before the very eyes of its readers. We know that Lily has embedded every story, every truth, with power, love, and wisdom for the ages, and we hope that all readers of this book, both now and in future generations, will feel and know the wisdom, the wit, and the love — the love of Lily!

About the Author

Beverley Bright Star did not always feel connected to Spirit. In fact, she felt quite the opposite in her early years. As a child growing up in the 1950's in Phoenix, Arizona, she felt extremely different and out of place, and wondered if there was something wrong with her. At the age of fourteen, she was contemplating becoming a nun after a brief but meaningful chance meeting with one in the courtyard at her church. A few days later, as she was standing at the back of the vestibule, she was startled to hear the words, "You can serve me in other ways" in her head. She knew then that Spirit was directing her to a different path. Fifteen months later, during a time of severe emotional upheaval and crisis, she cried out for God to change her life, as she could not go on in the same way anymore. At that moment she was touched by an angelic presence that stabilized and strengthened her life, and stayed with her.

After a painful marriage, she continued her search for truth and a deeper, more meaningful life. The emptiness, pain, and struggle drove her to go ever deeper within herself for answers. She explored different avenues and read many books, including the Edgar Cayce readings, the Kryon material, metaphysical books, Drunvalo Melchizadek's Flower of Life material, Paramahansa Yogananda's meditation lessons, sacred workshops, and a spiritual pilgrimage to France to heal the sacred feminine in the mid-90's.

But after that, a long desert period ensued for many years. Then, shortly before a severe health crisis in January 2011, she received a communication that brought her back to her path. It was only after a speedy recovery that she found her true spiritual purpose: channeling. During an instructional class by trance channel Cynthia Williams, 'Lily', the spirit entity from Sirius first channeled by Ruth Montgomery in the 1960's, came through to her, and she scribed the *Familial Integrity* book during a ninety-day period from April to July.

Beverly has more recently been working with, and channeling, Isis.

THE ANCIENT SECRET OF THE FLOWER OF LIFE VOLUME 2

- The Unfolding of the Third Informational System
- Whispers from Our Ancient Heritage
- Unveiling the Mer-Ka-Ba Meditation
- Using Your Mer-Ka-Ba
- Connecting to the Levels of Self
- Two Cosmic Experiments
- What We May Expect in the Forthcoming Dimensional Shift

$25.00 Softcover, 252 p.

ISBN 978-1-891824-21-0

The sacred Flower of Life pattern, the primary geometric generator of all physical form, is explored in even more depth in this volume, the second half of the famed Flower of Life workshop. The proportions of the human body, the nuances of human consciousness, the sizes and distances of the stars, planets, and moons, and even the creations of humankind, are all shown to reflect their origins in this beautiful and divine image. Through an intricate and detailed geometrical mapping, Drunvalo Melchizedek shows how the seemingly simple design of the Flower of Life contains the genesis of our entire third-dimensional existence.

From the pyramids and mysteries of Egypt to the new race of Indigo children, Drunvalo presents the sacred geometries of the reality and the subtle energies that shape our world. We are led through a divinely inspired labyrinth of science and stories, logic and coincidence, on a path of remembering where we come from and the wonder and magic of who we are.

Finally, for the first time in print, Drunvalo shares the instructions for the Mer-Ka-Ba meditation, step-by-step techniques for the re-creation of the energy field of the evolved human, which is the key to ascension and the next dimensional world. If done from love, this ancient process of breathing prana opens up for us a world of tantalizing possibility in this dimension, from protective powers to the healing of oneself, of others, and even of the planet.

BOOKS BY TOM T. MOORE

THE GENTLE WAY

A SELF-HELP GUIDE FOR THOSE WHO BELIEVE IN ANGELS

This book is for all faiths and beliefs with the only requirement being a basic belief in angels. It will put you back in touch with your guardian angel or strengthen and expand the connection that you may already have. How can I promise these benefits? Because I have been using these concepts for over ten years, and I can report these successes from direct knowledge and experience. But this is a self-help guide, so that means it requires your active participation.

CHAPTER TITLES

- Angels
- How I Began
- Easy Steps
- Home Life
- Politics
- Travel
- The Radiant Effect
- Living Prayers
- "I Hope" Requests

$14.95

140 PP. SOFTCOVER

ISBN 978-1-891824-60-9

THE GENTLE WAY II

BENEVOLENT OUTCOMES: THE STORY CONTINUES

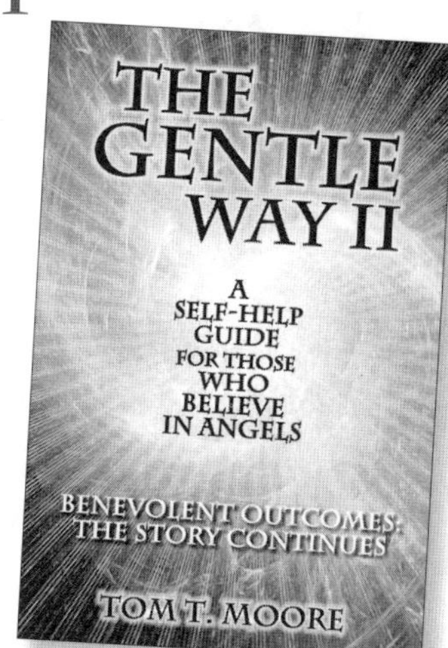

You'll be amazed at how easy it is to be in touch with guardian angels and how much assistance you can receive simply by asking. This inspirational self-help book, written for all faiths and beliefs, will explain how there is a more benevolent world that we can access, and how we can achieve this.

These very unique and incredibly simple techniques assist you in manifesting your goals easily and effortlessly for the first time. It works quickly, sometimes with immediate results — no affirmations, written intentions, or changes in behavior are needed. You don't even have to believe in it for it to work!

TOPICS INCLUDE:

- Safe Travel
- Your Home
- Your Work
- Medical Issues
- Home Finances
- Your Pets
- Work Relationships
- Personal Relationships

$16.95

273 PP. SOFTCOVER

ISBN 978-1-891824-80-7

Phone: 928-526-1345 or 1-800-450-0985 • Fax: 923-714-1132

Shamanic Secrets Mastery Series

Speaks of Many Truths and Reveals the Mysteries through Robert Shapiro

This book explores the heart and soul connection between humans and Earth. Through that intimacy, miracles of healing and expanded awareness can flourish. To heal the planet and be healed as well, we can lovingly extend our energy selves out to the mountains and rivers and intimately bond with the Earth. Gestures and vision can activate our hearts to return us to a healthy, caring relationship with the land we live on. The character of some of Earth's most powerful features is explored and understood, with exercises given to connect us with those places. As we project our love and healing energy there, we help the Earth to heal from human destruction of the planet and its atmosphere. Dozens of photographs, maps, and drawings assist the process in twenty-five chapters, which cover the Earth's more critical locations.

498 PP. $19.95 ISBN 978-1-891824-12-8

Learn to understand the sacred nature of your own physical body and some of the magnificent gifts it offers you. When you work with your physical body in these new ways, you will discover not only its sacredness, but how it is compatible with Mother Earth, the animals, the plants, and even the nearby planets, all of which you now recognize as being sacred in nature. It is important to feel the value of oneself physically before you can have any lasting physical impact on the world. If a physical energy does not feel good about itself, it will usually be resolved; other physical or spiritual energies will dissolve it because they are unnatural. The better you feel about your physical self when you do the work in the previous book, as well as this one and the one to follow, the greater and more lasting will be the benevolent effect on your life, on the lives of those around you, and ultimately on your planet and universe.

544 PP. $25.00 ISBN 978-1-891824-29-6

Spiritual mastery encompasses many different means to assimilate and be assimilated by the wisdom, feelings, flow, warmth, function, and application of all beings in your world that you will actually contact in some way. A lot of spiritual mastery has been covered in different bits and pieces throughout all the books we've done. My approach to spiritual mastery, though, will be as grounded as possible in things that people on Earth can use — but it won't include the broad spectrum of spiritual mastery, like levitation and invisibility. I'm trying to teach you things that you can actually use and benefit from. My life is basically going to represent your needs, and it gets out the secrets that have been held back in a storylike fashion, so that it is more interesting."

—Speaks of Many Truths through Robert Shapiro

676 PP. $29.95 ISBN 978-1-891824-58-6

DAVID K. MILLER

BIORELATIVITY: Planetary Healing Technologies

Biorelativity describes telepathic communication between humans and the spirit of Earth. The goal is to influence the outcome of natural Earth events, such as volcanoes and earthquakes.

$16.95 336 pp. Softcover 978-1891824-98-2

Kaballah and the Ascension

Miller explains how studying the Kaballah allows for a unique understanding of the concept of higher consciousness.

$16.95 176 pp. Softcover 978-1-891824-82-1

Raising the Spiritual Light Quotient

The concept of raising the spiritual light quotient is similar to the intelligence quotient used in modern psychology, the IQ test.

$16.95 416 pp. Softcover 978-1-891824-89-0

Connecting with the Arcturians

Many have talked about the ascension process, but few really understand what it means. This book easily answers all of your questions.

$17.00 240 pp. Softcover 978-1-891824-94-4

New Spiritual Technology for the Fifth-Dimensional Earth

Featured is information about native ceremonies to connect to Earth healing energies, thought projections, and thought communication.

$19.95 230 pp. Softcover 978-1-891824-79-1

Teachings from the Sacred Triangle

David offers the reader an understanding of the soul, soul evolution, and how the human species is advancing toward the next evolutionary step.

$22.00 292 pp. Softcover 978-0-971589-43-8

New Arcturian Perspectives for Planet Earth

This book represents the spiritual evolution of Earth and how it became part of the galactic hierarchy. There are many things that are happening in this part of the galaxy where Earth is. This means that a clearing or purification is going to happen to Earth, but not at the end of the calendar.

Teachings from the Sacred Triangle, Vol. 2

$16.95 254 pp. Softcover 978-1-891824-19-7

Teachings from the Sacred Triangle, Vol. 3

$16.95 254 pp. Softcover 978-1-891824-23-4

OUT-OF-BODY EXPERIENCES

by Gene Schmitz

WITH CHANNELED EXPLANATIONS AND COMMENTARY THROUGH Robert Shapiro

This book not only tells the full story of Gene's life, but it also includes a detailed conversation with an angelic being who speaks through superchannel Robert Shapiro to reveal the meaning behind Gene's out-of-body experiences and his life's purpose. In the process of explaining the twists and turns of Gene's life, this angelic being also unveils some surprising truths about the connection between the body and the soul that apply to all of us.

$14.95 Plus Shipping

ISBN 978-1-891824-95-1
Softcover 144 pp.
6 X 9 Perfect Bound

CHAPTERS INCLUDE:

- Soul Travel Begins
- Soul Travel Continues
- The White Light
- Floating Farther From Home
- My Soul Travels Resume
- Message from Grandpa
- Angels and Animals
- New Traveling Companions
- Soul Crossings

Hearing the Angels Sing:

A True Story of Angelic Assistance

by Peter Sterling

Hearing the Angel's Sing chronicles my extraordinary journeys into the higher dimensions of light where I met the angels who ultimately brought me to the realization that my mission was to be a channel for God's heavenly music. The book includes never-before-shared details of my journey of awakening. From the snowcapped peaks of the Rocky Mountains to the tropical jungles of the Mayan temple lands, the red rock towers of Sedona, and ultimately to the Incan highlands of Peru, this is a captivating story that will take you on an amazing journey of discovery!

—Peter Sterling

$16.95 Plus Shipping

ISBN 13: 978-1-891824-96-8
Softcover 218 pp.
6 X 9 Perfect Bound

CHAPTERS INCLUDE:

- Descension and Birth
- Down the Rabbit Hole
- Windows to Heaven
- Rocky Mountain High
- Angels and Devils
- Harmonic Converging
- Red Rocks Calling
- To Hear the Angels Sing
- Fires of Purification

Light Technology PUBLISHING

SHINING THE LIGHT BOOK SERIES

THROUGH ROBERT SHAPIRO

A CLOSER LOOK AT THE SERIES

The most significant events in Earth's history are happening in secret. Despite official denial and tactics of derision, inquiring minds are demanding the truth. This truth is stranger than all the fictions about ETs, alien bases, and the secret government. World-renowned authors Robert Shapiro, Tom Dongo, Dorothy Roeder, Arthur Fanning, Lyssa Royal-Holt, and Lee Carroll shed some light on these controversial and misunderstood topics. The battle in the heavens has begun. Become aware of the truth and don't get lost in the drama. Be the light that you are and you will be forever free.

THE BATTLE BEGINS!

This courageous book shines the light to expose truths that will change forever how we view our lives on this planet. It asks the reader to join in the investigations, ask the questions, and think the unthinkable. Explore the truth about the controllers of Earth and their alien allies. Discover the updated news about what is happening on the third dimension and what it means from the higher dimensions' perspective.

$12.95, 193 PP. Softcover
ISBN 13: 978-0-929385-66-2

THE BATTLE CONTINUES

This book continues the story of the secret government and alien involvement as well as information about the photon belt, cosmic holograms photographed in the sky, a new vortex forming near Sedona, and nefarious mining on the sacred Hopi land. Learn the current status of the secret government and those who want to usurp its power. Discover actual cosmic photographs of hidden crafts, beings, and events. The truth becomes even stranger as the story of alien involvement in Earth history continues.

$14.95, 418 PP. Softcover
ISBN 13: 978-0-929385-70-9

HUMANITY GETS A SECOND CHANCE

The focus shifts from the dastardly deeds of the secret government to humanity's role in creation. Earth receives unprecedented aid from Creator and cosmic councils, who recently lifted us beyond the third dimension to avert a great catastrophe. Humanity begins to learn to render the Sinister Secret Government powerless by being the light that it is.

$14.95, 460 PP. Softcover
ISBN 13: 978-0-929385-71-6

Visit our online bookstore: www.LightTechnology.com

Humanity's Greatest Challenge

The fourth installment of the series tells of the incredible vehicle traveling with the Hale-Bopp Comet — four times the size of Earth and filled with lightbeings. The book also covers the Montauk project, the HAARP project, and the uncreation of Hitler. Here are forty-nine more chapters in the ongoing process of shining the light on history as it happens — the real truth behind the scenes.

$14.95, 557 pp. Softcover
ISBN 13: 978-0-929385-93-8

Humanity Is Going to Make It!

Zoosh and others blast the cover off past events and hidden forces at work on this planet and reveal opportunities for immense growth and power. This is a pivotal time as the secrets and mysteries that have long bewildered humanity are at last illuminated by the light of truth.

$14.95, 320 pp. Softcover
ISBN 13: 978-1-891824-00-5

The End of What Was . . .

In this book, the mentors of humanity continue to expose the Sinister Secret Government's nefarious dealings, but they give us step-by-step instructions in the ancient and lost arts of benevolent magic — spiritual wizardry. This enables us as creators in training to blend our hearts, minds, and souls to become creators of our own destinies and thwart the Sinister Secret Government's goals.

$14.95, 316 pp. Softcover
ISBN 13: 978-1-891824-24-1

The First Alignment: World Peace

This edition focuses on the first alignment and what we can do to bring light and benevolence to humanity and Mother Earth. The objective is to move through — not jump over — the impossible solutions that have no logical means to explain them. In other words, the solution is located directly in the continuity of your immortal personalities.

$24.95, 521 pp. Softcover
ISBN 13: 978-1-891824-55-5

Shining the Light Book Series

Through Robert Shapiro

Phone: 928-526-1345 or 1-800-450-0985 • Fax: 928-714-1132

SEDONA

Journal of EMERGENCE!

Rated Number One!

We Offer Answers to Satisfy the Heart and to Inspire Lives!

YOU ARE EXPERIENCING AN UNPRECEDENTED EXPANSION into a new reality and a dimensional shift into a new state of being. This movement from one dimension to another while in a physical body has never been done before—it feels like you are building the rocket you're riding while it is blasting off!

THERE ARE NO ANCIENT BOOKS, NO RULEBOOKS, no manuals or procedures, no record of how to do this thing, because it has never been done before. During previous dimensional shifts, embodied beings would die in the old reality and then be reborn in the new one in new bodies with a different vibrational frequency.

SO LIGHTBEINGS, THROUGH THEIR CHANNELS, EXPLAIN THIS PROCESS and offer guidance and spiritual techniques to help you learn to feel and express love and benevolence–and to encourage you to change your behavior to ensure that the Earth remains habitable while you expand into your natural self and awaken to your natural talents and abilities. As this happens, you will allow yourself to flow with all humanity into a more benevolent version of Earth—into another dimensional focus, another of the strata of this existence.

The Sedona Journal of EMERGENCE! is the one monthly magazine readers never throw away.

ELECTRONIC SUBSCRIPTIONS available for SJE!

$29⁰⁰/Year for 12 months anywhere on the Planet! **$55⁰⁰** for 2 years!

Must be puchased online at: www.sedonajournal.com for you to obtain a user name and password.

Get the latest channeling and astrology 2 weeks before it is available on the newsstand.

Get SPECIAL UPDATES of channeled material before they're available on the newsstand with ELECTRONIC SUBSCRIPTIONS!

SEDONA Journal of EMERGENCE!

ORDER NOW!

TO RECEIVE SPECTACULAR SAVINGS!

ORDER ONLINE!
SAVE expensive freight or postage on your *Sedona Journal* subscription

We are now making ELECTRONIC SUBSCRIPTIONS available for the *SEDONA JOURNAL of EMERGENCE!*

We have now added content that will not fit into the printed magazine!

- Get the entire Journal online by subscription—and get it 2 weeks before it goes on the newsstand!
- Save on expensive freight or postage on your Sedona Journal subscription!

Electronic Subscriptions

❒ 1 yr. . . . $29 ❒ 2 yrs. . . . $55

All Electronic and Combo Subscriptions *MUST* be purchased online at: www.sedonajournal.com to obtain username and password

Get the Best of Both Worlds! Special Combo Offers!

U.S.A

Get a Printed Subscription Along with an Electronic Subscription - U.S.A. only

1st Class ❒ 1 yr. . . $82 ❒ 2 yrs. . . $159
2nd Class ❒ 1 yr. . . $59 ❒ 2 yrs. . . $109

Canada & Mexico

Get an Airmail Printed Subscription Along with an Electronic Subscription for only

❒ 1 yr. . . . $95 ❒ 2 yrs. . . . $179

NOTE: The U.S. Postal Service has changed postal rates, eliminating Canadian 2nd Class Surface and increasing all airmail rates.

All Countries
Except U.S.A., Canada, & Mexico

Get an Airmail Printed Subscription Along with an Electronic Subscription for only

❒ 1 yr. . . . $152 ❒ 2 yrs. . . . $285

NOTE: The U.S. Postal Service has changed postal rates, eliminating global 2nd Class Surface and increasing all airmail rates.

---

yes! Send Me:

Printed and Mailed Subcriptions

1ST CLASS	2ND CLASS
❒ 2 yrs. $129	❒ 2 yrs. $79
❒ 1 yr. $65	❒ 1 yr. $43

USA

AIR

CANADA & MEXICO

❒ 2 yrs (24 issues) $149
❒ 1 yr (12 issues). $79

U.S. dollars only

NOTE: The U.S. Postal Service has changed postal rates, eliminating Canadian 2nd Class Surface and increasing all airmail rates.

AIR

ALL COUNTRIES Except USA, Canada & Mexico

❒ 2 yrs (24 issues) $255
❒ 1 yr (12 issues). $136

U.S. dollars only

NOTE: The U.S. Postal Service has changed postal rates, eliminating global 2nd Class Surface and increasing all airmail rates.

My Name ____________________
Address ____________________
City ____________________ State: ______
Zip: ____________________ Phone ______
Email ____________________
Gift Recipient Name ____________________
Address ____________________
City ____________________ State: ______
Zip: ____________________
Personalized Gift Card from ____________________
METHOD OF PAYMENT:
❒ CHECK # ❒ M.O.
❒ VISA ❒ MASTERCARD ❒ NOVUS ❒ AMEX
CARD NO. ____________________
EXPIRATION DATE ____________________
SIGNATURE ____________________

Phone: 928-526-1345 or 1-800-450-0985 • Fax: 923-714-1132

Light Technology PUBLISHING

EASY ORDER 24 HOURS A DAY

1 Order ONLINE!

www.lighttechnology.com

Email:
customersrv@
lighttechnology.net

2 Order by Mail

Send To:
Light Technology Publishing
PO Box 3540
Flagstaff, AZ 86003

3 Order by Phone

800-450-0985
928-526-1345

4 Order by Fax

928-714-1132

Available from your favorite bookstore or:

LIGHT Technology PUBLISHING

MasterCard · VISA · AMERICAN EXPRESS · NOVUS

Visit Our Websites!

- Shopping Cart w/ Secure Transactions
- In-Depth Information on Books, Including Excerpts and Contents
- Use our Great Links to Other Sites

- Read Excerpts of Monthly Channeling and Predictions in Advance
- Use Our Email Links to Contact Us or Send a Submission
- Electronic Subscriptions Available—With or Without Print Copies

Learn the techniques of benevolence toward self and benevolence toward others and you will create global peace. Download all the techniques of benevolent magic and living prayer for FREE!

All of humanity constitutes the Explorer Race, volunteers for a grand and glorious experiment. Discover your purpose, your history and your future. Download the first chapter of each book for FREE!

What we call shamanism is the natural way of life for beings on other planets. Learn to be aware of your natural self and your natural talents and abilities. Download the first chapter of each book for FREE!

Visit our online bookstore: www.LightTechnology.com